G OF ENGLAND

lor Dynasty

STEWART

F YORK

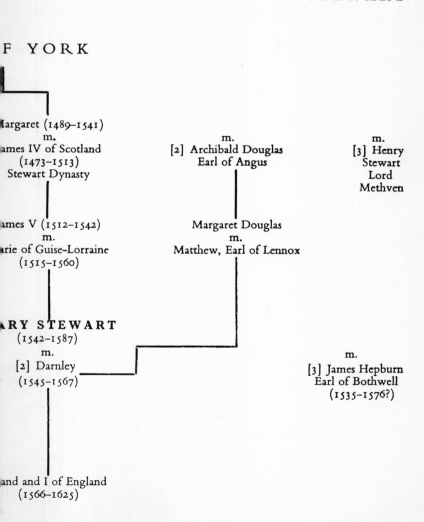

Margaret (1489–1541)
m.
James IV of Scotland
(1473–1513)
Stewart Dynasty

m.
[2] Archibald Douglas
Earl of Angus

m.
[3] Henry
Stewart
Lord
Methven

James V (1512–1542)
m.
Marie of Guise-Lorraine
(1515–1560)

Margaret Douglas
m.
Matthew, Earl of Lennox

MARY STEWART
(1542–1587)
m.
[2] Darnley
(1545–1567)

m.
[3] James Hepburn
Earl of Bothwell
(1535–1576?)

and and I of England
(1566–1625)

MARY
QUEEN OF SCOTS

Mary, Queen of Scots
By an Unknown Artist
Devonshire Collection, Hardwick Hall (National Trust)

N. BRYSSON MORRISON

MARY
Queen of Scots

NEW YORK

· THE VANGUARD PRESS · INC ·

PEARL MORE SMIETON
Her Book

CONTENTS

❋

LIST OF ILLUSTRATIONS

BOOK ONE

Spring

December 1542 – August 1561

CHAPTER ONE

And there looms, on the marge
Of the river, a barge
That nobody roweth or steereth.

M ARY, QUEEN OF SCOTS, was born on the 8th December,
1542, at Linlithgow Palace, and was executed at Fotheringay on the 8th February, 1587. Within the compass of these
forty-five years, a tidal wave of change shook Europe. Because
she was a queen, she took the shock of the tumult. Because she
was the woman she was, she contributed to the happenings
around her. Her story is what it is because of her involuntary
reaction to the influences that pulled, the biases she withstood
and the principles to which she adhered.

Volcanic ground is always fertile ground, but those who lived
in Mary's century were aware only of the explosions that rocked
their world. Yet, for all its storminess, there is, viewing her story
from this distance, little disorder about the scene, no confusion
in the events. Instead something like pattern emerges, for time
does not so much spotlight the past as act like a lens through
which it is seen in perspective. As we look back at this woman
taking her place in history, it is seen that she and she alone
could have been Mary Stewart.

Her personal motto, that which she inherited from her French
mother, was 'In my End is my Beginning'. With her biography
we have to reverse her motto, to begin at the beginning, towards
the end of the year 1542, Fotheringay a far cry away.

Her father, James V, was approaching thirty-one and had been

King of Scotland for twenty-nine of these years. This precipitate inheritance of their kingdom in infancy was symbolic of the
Stewarts. The daughter of Robert the Bruce brought the
crown to their house, and she was born after the death of her
mother. James's father was killed at Flodden, that fatal battle
which should never have been lost and from which Scotland was
not to recover, the battle-field which claimed the flowers of the
forest and which buried the Golden Age, bright as a shield, of
medieval Scottish history.

Mary was to inherit her father's red-gold hair, his oval face,
the heavy Stewart lids and the Stewart blood, with its mixture
of charm and passion, the recklessness of those who 'gang their
ain gait', its wayward weakness allied to great nobility, and its
undiluted personal courage. With eleven centuries of royal descent behind her, she was swaddled in the birthright which
swaddled every Stewart before and after her, the divine right of
kings, and she shared their fatal inability to read men.

Her mother, Marie of Guise, was daughter of a noble French
house, a woman of composure and peculiar gifts, which had not
yet been brought into play. She had, with her French sense of
proportion, what most of the Stewarts lacked—staying power,
and this steadfastness acted like a sheath in which the glancing,
nimble blade of her husband's temperament could find repose.
Her daughter was to inherit through her the Guise height and,
from a family that had produced nuns, abbots, abbesses and
cardinals, devotion to the Roman Catholic faith.

As her mother was a young widow before she married James,
so her father was a widower before he married Marie. His first
bride had been French like his second, for he had refused the
hand of his English cousin, to be known later as Bloody Mary,
proffered by his uncle, Henry VIII. Nor did he accept the princess
he sailed to France to espouse, when he discovered on arrival

she was plain, deformed and an invalid. Instead he fell in love with the King's sixteen-year-old daughter.

They warned him she was too delicate to endure travail, but he married her in spite of them, for he came of a race of men who liked their own way and were strong enough to enforce it. He brought the French King's frail little daughter home and she knelt to kiss the soil of Scotland. Within a few swift weeks they had to shut her too bright eyes and cross her too thin hands.

His second marriage was not the love-match of his first: sons he must have, legitimate sons. Anne Boleyn had gone to the scaffold the year before and his uncle Henry was now in a position to enter the marriage lists. The English King would have liked well the tall young widow who had been born Marie of Guise. He said he was big and needed a big wife, but Marie laughingly replied her neck was slender and chose instead the younger man, the handsome King of Scots. Henry was tactlessly offered by the French King the princess his nephew had rejected. The relationship between England and Scotland, never harmonious even when family ties were not involved, was perilously strained.

They were two nations, two different races of men, sharing the one small island. The nearer the neighbour the deadlier can be the feud. France was Scotland's old ally, her old enemy England over the Border, with whom she had always rejected alliance that did not safeguard her independence as a separate kingdom. If the Scot's great weakness was his inability to co-operate, it was also his strength, because had he been able to do so, Scotland would have been assimilated by her more powerful neighbour (her population was approximately one-tenth of that of England's), or become an appanage of France.

The first sight Marie had of her new country was the spires, towers and battlements of St. Andrews, the Vatican of Scotland. It was said Henry sent out pirate ships to capture her, but Marie landed safely on the red earth of Fife, where the wind scraped through the place-names.

Scotland had reached the zenith of its recognition as a European state and St. Andrews was at the height of its glory. A thriving seaport, it was not only a cathedral city but the home of the first Scots university. The Catholic Church had founded it over a century ago to consolidate their position with learning. Heretics, and everyone who was not a Catholic was a heretic, were beginning to question those who held by bell, book and candle.

For even in Scotland, the farthest out-post of Europe, lights had been burning, not with the flickering of taper or candle but with the flare and flame of certain bonfire, as the Holy Catholic Kirk strove to stamp out the heresies of those who spoke of the Word of God instead of listening to the voice of the Church.

Fortunately for the Church, the uncompromising records of God's dealings with man were safely locked up in the Greek and Latin tongues, which few could read. Translation of the Bible was forbidden—the Catholic Church dare not let the people read a Book which taught that all men were equal in the sight of God. An Englishman, one Tyndale, had defied that ban and translated the New Testament. Clattering printing-presses in Germany produced copies after he had been imprisoned, strangled and burnt for heresy; and sturdy traders from Leith, Dundee and Montrose were smuggling it into Scotland hidden in bales of cloth.

It had been prophesied ten years ago when Patrick Hamilton, the first Scots reformer, was burnt in this sea-stormed town, that the smoke from him would infect as many as it blew upon. But as yet the powerful Roman Catholic Church was little perturbed, unaware of the existence of an insignificant notary called John Knox in Haddington.

No one who watched the marriage of James to Marie of Guise, celebrated with solemn pomp that June day, was aware that they were witnessing the last King's wedding in Scotland.

Next morning the new Queen visited all the kirks and colleges in the town with its high, crow-stepped buildings. She had that replenishing vitality her daughter was to have, which charmed as it was charmed. She exclaimed to the King that she had been told in France Scotland was a barbarous country, desolate of all pleasant commodities, but now she saw with her own eyes exactly the opposite. Never, she declared, had she seen more pleasing men and women in so little room as she saw that day.

The rejoicings lasted for six weeks, the friendly challenge of joust and tournament, the cheer of banquet and pageant. Then the French wedding-guests sailed back to France, and the King and Queen proceeded to Falkland, which James was transforming from a hunting-lodge into a pleasure palace to delight a bride. Always there was music at court, Italian minstrels, viol-players, trumpeters and drummers.

He carried his consort to Stirling, and from the rocky height of its castle she saw what looked like the whole of his kingdom mapped below her gaze. Magnificence meant as much to Stewart as it did to Guise. It was Linlithgow that impressed Marie above all. She, who knew the great houses of France, said when she came to Linlithgow that never had she seen a more princely palace. They reached Edinburgh, the smallest, the most crowded, the most turbulent capital in Europe, and the Queen made her public entry on St. Margaret's Day. The procession entered by the West Port, up the West Bow, and down the Royal Way to the new palace of Holyrood. Behind her, riding between earth and sky, was a castle so old it was merged into the rock it crowned.

Throughout their progress the people welcomed her because of the man who rode at her side. The Stewarts' traditional allies were France, the Church and the common people; but James V meant even more to the common people than had most of their sovereigns. He was known as the poor man's king and they had their own familiar name for him, the Gude-man. Perhaps it was the long years of his captive youth that made him like to join them in disguise at their fairs and markets and merry-makings. It was only when the dance was stilled and the music silenced that they wondered about the identity of the red-bearded stranger no longer in their midst.

Now they rejoiced for him when they saw his Queen. She was strong, which meant there would be princes and princesses to take the place of his many chance-bairns. James, unlike most of the Stewart kings, was profligate, but they had not been deliberately corrupted as he had been when a boy by his step-father.

No good ever crossed the Border from England and the King's mother had been an ill wind to Scotland once her lord his father died. With her marriages and divorces she had proved herself out of the same stable as her brother Henry now filling the English throne.

The people thought what James thought about the nobility: the deil take them. He had the same fight against them that all his fathers had had before him. The nobles, and his mother had made the strongest of them his step-father, had fought for the possession of their boy king, because whoever held him held power. Now he was grown he ruled for himself without fear or favour, but the only counter he had to keep the nobility in check was the Church. That was not to say he was blind to its failings. He swore that the good would be suffered and the evil reformed in Scotland if, by God's grace, he were granted life to do it. But his Protestant uncle Henry had failed to induce him to break with Rome. The suggestion that he should imburse himself by spoiling the monasteries struck James as blasphemous, although like most he liked well to be rich.

The common people of Scotland were inquisitive, combative and noisy with talk: 'the man hath more words than the master.' They said what they thought without let or hindrance. An English ambassador wrote to his sovereign Henry of the 'beastly liberty' the Scots enjoyed. And they were beginning to deride a Church that neglected and oppressed them, for there was nothing in it for the poor it mulcted with tithes. They ceased to attend its services, until the priests complained there was no longer a living to be made out of Mass. Excommunication, the dread Cursing of earlier days, had become a jest and a mockery.

The Guise were a united family and letters with gossip and news linked Marie, the eldest of ten children, to her home circle. Her mother never wrote but she mentioned the little son Marie had borne to her first husband and whom she had to leave behind in France. He wrote to his mother himself when he was old enough, enclosing in his letter a piece of string to let her see how tall he had grown. Did Marie think of the child she could not have beside her when she saw her husband's eldest son and daughter by the Lady of Lochleven who, above his other illegitimate children, were raised to almost princely rank?

An heir to the crown was born at St. Andrews, and Marie's Cardinal uncle wrote that the French King was as pleased at the news of the prince's birth as if it had been his own. A second son was born at Falkland the following year. Within a week of his birth tragedy struck when both baby princes, one at Falkland and the other at Stirling, died within a few days of each other.

James began to show signs of his grandfather's melancholy, and could not sleep. When he stayed at Linlithgow his nights were haunted by terrifying dreams.

Four years after his marriage the clouds that had been threatening broke into open warfare between England and Scotland. James's disaffected nobles refused to support him when the tide of battle could have turned in his favour. Another army was pro-

vided by the Church and the King marched west, where he fell
ill.

It was November, too late for warfare, but James may well
have reasoned that it was better to use an army when he had
one to use. Too sick to lead the men himself, he made the disastrous decision of sending them forward into enemy country.
More disastrous, he gave a young favourite, Oliver Sinclair, a
secret commission to take command as soon as they crossed the
river Esk. He may have thought in his absence he could count
on the loyalty of a personal friend as he had been unable to
depend on his nobles when he was present.

The Scottish force crossed the Esk during the night. The men
believed the King was with them and only discovered he was
not when day broke over the flats of the treacherous Solway
Moss. Lord Maxwell, as Warden of the Marches, was entitled to
lead, but Sinclair produced the King's commission, and his soldiers raised him as general of the forces on a platform of spears.
Maxwell's men sided with their master and into the confusion
rode an English force a quarter their number.

This had none of the glory and heart-breaking heroism of
Flodden. This was panic, rout, abject defeat. Amongst the hun-
dreds of prisoners taken by the English were numbered Lord
Maxwell and Sir Oliver Sinclair.

News of the disaster was brought to the sick King at Loch-
maben, who must have felt nightmare had become reality. We
have a picture of him riding from place to place like a spectre
through winter mists. He came to Sir James Kirkcaldy's house
and told his lady he would not live to see Christmas Day. He
kept calling out, 'Fled Oliver? Fie Oliver!' as though he hoped
the very horror of it might waken him from his nightmare. At
last he reached Falkland, the little summer palace surrounded by
forests, where he had loved to hunt, now gaunt and bare with
winter.

It was there they brought him the tidings that the Queen, lying at Linlithgow, was safely delivered. As though the pause that followed bred in him some sudden suspicion, he stirred where he lay to demand:

'A man-child or a woman?'

An eternity passed before the reply came.

'A fair daughter.'

The words hit him like blows and he cried out as if struck:

'The deil go with it! The deil go with it! Adieu, farewell. It came with a lass, and it will pass with a lass.'

So saying he sank back and turned his face to the wall.

He spoke little from that time. Six days later, at midnight, 'he turned him back and looked and beheld all his lords about him, and gave a little smile and laughter, then kissed his hand and offered the same to all his lords round about him, and thereafter held up his hands to God and yielded the spirit.'

Thus he died, this King whose life stretched between two lost battles. The daughter he never saw became queen before she was a week old.

CHAPTER TWO

Be she young, or be she old,
All in French garlands,
It's for a bride she must be sold,
And adieu to you, my darling.

THERE is a rare chivalry in a letter from the English Warden of the Marches written within a few days of the Scots King's death. He tells his ruler Henry that he has called off a raid on Duns as he considered it was not to his majesty's honour that his soldiers should make war or invade upon a dead body or upon a young widow or on a suckling, her daughter. In the same letter the soldier urges his royal master to annex south Scotland with the words, 'If we hold hard, all will be ours.'

But Henry saw in the birth of his great-niece at her father's death providence working for him, and he seized the opportunity in his impatient hands. There was another process now than costly warfare by which the Scots crown could be seized—marriage. It had been tried before; each king who had sat on the English throne had attempted to subject Scotland through either conquest or marriage, but never had such a chance as this presented itself, with so many high-ranking prisoners to play their part in Henry's game. And throughout this game played without rules, he never lost sight of the ball, the small Scots Queen.

By the grace of God and his third wife Jane Seymour, he had a son and heir now, the five-year-old Edward. Union of marriage must be effected between the new born Queen and Prince Edward. He sold their freedom to the Solway prisoners on condition they agreed, on their return to Scotland, to have the child straightway delivered to his guardianship.

It is now that Marie as Queen Dowager, no longer shadowed by her sovereign, moves into the round to stand by herself. Loneliness and isolation cling to her figure as we look back on her. Her position, a widow in a foreign country whose child was queen, was fraught with peril, but few could have filled it as did she. Conciliatory, she played for time. A woman amongst men, she was mistress of whatever situation she found herself in and in diplomacy few were her master, skilful enough to achieve her own ends, custody of her child, without drawing attention to what she was about.

It was from her mother that Mary was to take her love of giving. After her husband's death, Marie adopted his illegitimate daughter, augmenting her dowry, and endowing her brother. She was brave, with the courage of endurance, yet she fainted at the sight of blood. And we have a foresight of the daughter when we read in the old chronicles of the mother, so transported with joy at the news of victory, that she must leap on a horse to ride down to the camp, to thank not only the commanders but the soldiers.

She ordered her household well, as became the daughter of a great family who had been brought up with careful simplicity, and nothing she did gave rise to scandal. The Earl of Lennox and the Earl of Bothwell were both her suitors, but she said since she had been a king's wife, her heart was too high to look any lower. Already fate was beginning to weave curious patterns round the infant daughter she would not allow to be removed from her room. When she was grown, Mary was to marry Darnley and James Hepburn, the sons of the two men who had wooed her mother.

With her unusual characteristics of adaptability, her masculine grasp of affairs and her woman's tact, Marie was admirably fitted to fill the position of Regent. She was fond of her adopted country; Scotland probably meant more to her than it ever was to mean to her daughter, and she had the tolerance and magnanimity which make for good government. But Scots law decreed that the heir-presumptive, during a sovereign's minority, should be the Regent or Governor. It was an unfortunate law in this case, when the minor was a girl and the heir-presumptive the Earl of Arran. Wavering as candle-flame in draught, he was more dangerous as ally than adversary because of his weakness, with the vaulting ambition that often accompanies it.

The best the Solway lords could achieve for the English King was that Mary should be espoused to Edward, and sent to England in her tenth year. Henry had to modify his demands, which he did with a poor grace. Both sides knew a lot could happen in ten years: a lot was to happen in ten weeks. The Scots saw to it that the marriage treaty left no loophole for annexation: their country must ever have and bear the name of Scotland, and enjoy the same old liberty, privileges and freedom it had enjoyed since time began.

Although the treaty was signed, no one in Scotland liked it. One nobleman voiced what all were thinking when he remarked, 'I dislike not so much the marriage as the manner of the wooing.' The English envoy was told that Scotland was a stout nation and would never agree to have an Englishman as their king, that even if the whole nobility of the realm consented to it, the common people, and the stones in the street, would rise up and rebel.

Like most dictators, Henry was not noted for his patience. Hardly was the ink dry on the marriage and peace treaties than he seized a rich fleet of Scots merchant-ships and broke the truce further by aggression in Teviotdale. The Scots turned on the Governor, whom they accused of colouring a peace to their undoing and selling their Queen. The English envoy escaped only in the nick of time when the house where he lodged was set on fire by the Edinburgh populace. He wrote to Henry complaining of their malice, concluding with the remark that he would rather be among Turks.

The Governor, intimidated by unpopularity, hastily arranged the coronation of the Queen. The ceremony, performed with crown, sceptre, sword and baby in Stirling, exacerbated Henry. The Scots declared the English treaties null and void, and renewed their ancient alliance with France.

On the 24th January, 1544, when Mary was a year old, a first child was born, after nine years of marriage, to Henri of France and his wife Catherine de Medici. Because he was born in the midst of an eclipse of the sun, a special motto and device were adopted for him. The device was a lily, symbolic of a future sovereign of France, flanked by the sun and moon, with the motto, 'Between these I issued.'

Marie watched her daughter 'breed her teeth', recover from the smallpox, fall prey to the measles, in the manner of hundreds of children in croft and castle. She was sturdier than she seemed, for her skin, so fair and fine it bruised at little pressure, lent her a look of transparent frailty.

The child was hurried from one stronghold to another as Henry, determined to be her father-in-law, despatched the Earl of Hertford into Scotland to take her by force. His instructions, which were carried out to the letter, were to inflict all the misery he could, lay waste the country, seize Edinburgh and put to fire and sword man, woman and child. Leith and Edinburgh fell and Hertford, the Scourge of the Scots, boasted he had desolated the country to within six miles of Stirling. Three times the Scourge invaded, leaving destruction and devastation in his wake. As the Rough Wooing burnt and ravaged Scotland, prayers for Mary to marry Edward were read in all English churches.

After the disastrous battle of Pinkie, which went down on the Scots calendar as Black Saturday, Mary was conveyed for greater security to the island sanctuary of Inchmahone on the Lake of Menteith. From there she could be hurried if need be into the fastness of the Highlands where even the English could not find her.

The quiet black-robed canons in their tree-embowered priory found themselves hosts to the Scottish court. Amongst those accompanying the Queen Dowager and her daughter were the child's nurse, her tutors, governess, Lord Keeper and four small companions. These children were wisely chosen by Marie, member of a large family, to be brought up with her daughter that she might not be lonely, and become her maids of honour. All were of noble Scots birth, the same age as their royal companion and bore her name of Mary. They were Mary Beaton, Mary Seton, Mary Livingstone and Mary Fleming.

There was no Mary Hamilton or Mary Carmichael of the well-known song. The lives of the four Maries, each piquant with her own personality, lace themselves in and out of the Queen's story with the blessedness of everyday, and call for no embroidery by ballad-monger. It says more for Mary than anything else that her personal servants, both high and humble, men and women, were devoted to her, chosing to share her captivity so that they could serve her through the stagnant years of lengthening age as they had served her in the dancing hours of her youth.

Men, not women, were to be this child's enemies. Even in the days of her infamy, no woman raised her voice against her to impute blame. It was men who turned on her, to vent their destructive hate where once they had worshipped; to defame, rend and tear apart. For she had that fascination like a fire that consumed men's love, the fatal fascination she inherited not from her mother but from the Stewarts.

In a country distracted and overrun, the Scots turned to their old ally; the Queen Mother, to the land of her birth. Negotiations were entered into for Mary to be sent to France, to be educated and brought up under the French King's care, and eventually to marry his son, the Dauphin, the little boy who had issued so providentially between the sun and the moon. Henri II promised to defend Scotland and to maintain her independence against the cruelty and arrogance of England, sending a force to drive the English troops out. The Scots agreed, laying down as their sole condition that the laws and liberties of their realm should be preserved inviolate.

We can read the relief of the mother overflowing in the letter Marie wrote to her brothers to tell them the Scots Estates (Parliament) had agreed to the proposals. Her gratitude was such that unconsciously it warmed and heightened actuality. 'Each consented to be subject to the said Lord (Henri II),' the Frenchwoman wrote, 'because of the honour he is doing the Queen, my daughter, in wishing her to marry his son.' Henri himself was under this quite mistaken impression; he looked upon himself 'as holding at present the place of King of Scotland, with the obedience of its vassals and subjects, who cannot henceforth have any other will than mine.' Fortunately the Scots, great lovers of minding their own business, were unaware they were anyone's vassals.

Marie was to write later that pain of the heart was the worst ill to bear. Even her relief that her child was in friendly hands could not assuage the pain she must have felt at her heart the day she watched, from Dumbarton Rock, the French galleys bear her away. Mary herself wept at the parting, but silently: already, not yet six, she was learning the restraint of royalty. She seems to have been both a lively and merry child, for of her large company she was the least ill on that boisterous voyage, and made fun of those who were.

Through the letters the mother received we have glimpses of Mary in these early years. The Guises were well pleased with her. The grandmother saw in the pretty child with her bright hair the makings of a beautiful girl: the shrewd eyes noted she was graceful and self-assured, as intelligent a child as one could see. The King, her future father-in-law, thought her the prettiest and most graceful little princess he had ever seen, and Catherine de Medici, the mother-in-law to be, remarked that the little Queen of Scots had but to smile to turn the heads of all Frenchmen.

Two years later, in one of those rare quiet periods when a truce between England, France and Scotland brought temporary respite, Marie sailed to her native country. She found the star of the house of Guise shining with a dazzling brilliance. The two young brothers she had left on her marriage to the Scots King were now reaching to these heights where one was to become known as the King and Pope of France, the other France's Sword and Shield.

The winter sped by happily, the days between Candlemas and Shrovetide proud with the splendour of procession and pageant and gay with masked balls. She met again the little son she had left behind when she went to Scotland, grown to tall sixteen now, who had promised his small half-sister to be her knight and fight all those who would hurt her. The joyousness of the long-looked-for meeting between mother and son sank into sorrow when in one of those sudden illnesses that struck down youth in those days, he died whilst she was with him.

When she said good-bye to her eight-year-old daughter at Fontainebleau, it was mercifully hidden from Marie that this was the last time she would see her.

She returned to Scotland, to spend the last nine years of her life guarding her daughter's throne, protecting her crown, upholding unpopular French policy whenever she could. For a country wearies of no guests so quickly as it wearies of its liberators; the ally usually over-stays his welcome.

Edinburgh was made jealous by Marie creating Leith a burgh. She realised its importance for commercial purposes as well as for a military port; also it was her nearest point of communication with France. Arran was bribed with the high-sounding title of Duke of Chatelherault and a French estate to give up the Regency, and her accession was brought about through her conciliation of the Protestants. But towards the end of her life they were in open insurrection against her. She wrote protesting that a letter they had sent her 'appeareth to us rather to have come from a Prince to his subjects, than from subjects to them that hath authority.'

The Protestants had now grown to be a power in the land, and it was no longer dangerous to be numbered with them. The mighty Roman Catholic Church had not yet fallen in Scotland, but behind her splendid façade she was crumbling. When she attempted to put her house in order, and in no other country of Europe did her abuses go to such lengths, she had not the energy or will to do so. Three times during these years Church Councils were held which passed statutes to remedy prevailing vices, yet neither redress nor amendment took place. Reformation had to come from outside, not within. The strength was in the supplanting church, not the supplanted; and the hearts of the common people were with the Reformers.

There were now two factions in Scotland: the 'English' party, Scots Protestants who favoured dealings with Protestant England, and the 'French' party loyal to the old alliance and the old faith. The English party was symbolised by those who called themselves the Lords of the Congregation, the French by that of the Queen Regent. There came a time when English troops were in Scotland helping the Congregation to try to drive out the French, and French troops assisting the Queen Regent in an effort to drive out the English. The common people, seeing their country made a battle-ground, wished a plague on both their houses, or as their own poet wittily put it:

> 'I cannot sing for the vexation
> Of Frenchmen and Congregation
> That have made trouble in the nation
> And many a bare bigging.
>
> I have no will to sing or dance,
> For fear of England and of France;
> God send them sorrow and mischance
> In case of their coming.'

As Regent, Marie reached the plenitude of her power. She moves through these years, in the exultation of victory and the humiliation of defeat, to her death in Edinburgh Castle, within earshot of gunfire. We see her in the pomp and ceremonial of Parliament, or setting forth in royal state on justiciary progress, building herself a mansion at Leith in order not to be cut off from France, and playing picquet through the long northern nights with her French lords.

CHAPTER THREE

Together let us sweetly live,
Together let us die,
And each a starry crown receive,
And reign above the sky.

Mary, animated and active, must have looked blooming in
the French King's nursery. All his children were sickly,
pallid. She blossomed where they drooped. And Francis, the
Dauphin, her bridegroom-to-be, was the most delicate of all, but
in his weak body there struggled a gallantry of spirit and something of his father's vitality. At three he refused to be dressed
any longer as a girl and he loved the suit of armour he was given
when he was seven.

He took at once to the forthcoming little girl who was to be
his bride: their affection for each other sprang from the spontaneous confidence of childhood. His future dependence on her
can be traced back to these early days when he liked to take her
by the hand and talk to her by herself. Mary was naturally loving,
and in their pleased acceptance of one another probably neither
child was aware of his defective speech.

As the years passed more listless olive-skinned babies joined
Mary, Francis and his two sisters, Ysabel and Claude, in the
royal children's establishment. Of Henri II and Catherine de
Medici's seven children who survived, three were to be crowned
King of France and one Queen of Spain.

As they move in their rich jewelled costumes, these children
throw long shadows. Charles, who died insane after authorising

the massacre of St. Bartholomew, liked having Bible stories read to him when he was small; and Henri, the queer peaked baby with high shoulders, was to have his account of murder paid back in kind by an assassin's dagger.

Mary's four Maries accompanied her to France, but her boon companion was Ysabel, the Dauphin's eldest sister. She was two and a half years younger, with none of the Scots Queen's brilliance or pre-eminence. But there can be great sweetness in a minor key, and instead of a shadow Ysabel left behind translucence in the memory of all she loved.

She and Mary shared the same household, as it was the French King's desire that they be brought up as sisters. Because she was a crowned Queen, with the power to grant pardons and set prisoners free, Mary was given precedence over his daughters. He assured the Estates of Scotland that nothing would be omitted to do her honour and he kept his promise. Scotland was valuable as an ally to France, and Henri looked upon the small Scots Queen not so much as a symbol of alliance as having brought her kingdom as a kind of free gift with her.

Naturally he was well disposed to this new acquisition to the royal nursery even before her arrival. But when he saw her he was charmed. He called her his little *reinette* of Scotland and wrote to her mother to give her the nursery tidings of one whom he described as 'my daughter and yours'. A tall handsome man, he lost all his taciturnity and was at his best with his children. They did not feel with him the restraint they felt with their mother.

Catherine de Medici was perhaps not so enamoured as she appeared with her future daughter-in-law. The house of Guise had been hateful to her from the beginning. She had always had to submerge her emotions since she, an Italian, had been greeted with covert contempt and ill-concealed sneers by the French court because her dowry had not come up to expectations. But as she wrote her prolific letters, her broad face brooding as a

peasant's, her hates grew in tortuous shapes like giant mush-
rooms in the cellar of her mind. It had been suggested, before
the birth of the Dauphin, that the King should divorce childless
Catherine de Medici and marry Mary of Guise. Now she was
the mother of seven children, four of them sons. With such
sureties for the future, she could afford to wait in the passive-
ness of the present. But sometimes she must have wondered
how long she would have to bide, if she would ever possess
power, instead of this existence of always having to subject herself to others' wills, of having to seem so pleased with everybody.

She watched the star of Guise ascending in popularity and
power: six sons to climb ever higher, and the two eldest the
most dangerous because they set the pace. The Duke of Guise,
soldier and hero, defender of Metz, with the war-scar on his
cheek which made the common people affectionately call him
Balafré. And the subtle churchman, the Cardinal of Lorraine,
scheming and assiduous behind his brother's shield, entrench-
ing, consolidating and building up their house. They were not
Frenchmen, they were Lorrainers, and Catherine knew that, compared to their own family, the King, the throne, France itself,
meant little to any of the name of Guise.

There was always someone to repeat the things that first
wounded, then inflamed. She had heard of the Cardinal's remark that the one child of the King who resembled him was
his daughter by his mistress Valentinois. She disliked the stately
churchman, grey before he was thirty, with his smooth delicate
speech, even more than she disliked his warrior brother, although
both had insulted her by the court they paid to Valentinois in
order to ingratiate themselves with the King. The niece was very
like her Cardinal uncle; the same air of elegancy clung to both.

Childhood as we know it did not exist in these days; children
were not so much boys and girls as small men and women, but
Mary shared with the French royal children that pristine state
when everything was new to them and the world they looked at

they saw for the first time. They would not notice the background of sumptuous palace and magnificent castle so much as their pets and favourite animals. The chateau of Madame Valentinois was full of delights, aviaries and fish-ponds, fountains and running streams. The hunt was sport for queens as well as kings. The sound of the dogs released from their kennels, the call of horn and the excited thud of horses' hooves were as much music in the ears of Mary Stewart as they were to the French royal brothers. The flagging Francis and Charles, in their adolescence, were to out-tire their most energetic followers. Mary astonished everyone when she arrived in France by dressing her pet falcon, casting it off and reclaiming it with her own hands.

Like many boys, Francis disliked lessons, but never wearied listening to tales of hunting and shooting and the game of war. No one could coax him to his books so skilfully as Mary. She was to continue to read Latin with her tutor even when she was married.

She and Ysabel with her four Maries learnt to make poetry, to play the harp, the lute, zithern and virginals, to knit in wools and silks, and, what she loved most, to embroider. Instead of the old-fashioned Gothic handwriting, she was taught the new Italian mode—the handwriting that was to be so easy to forge. As there was no W in the French language, she spelled her name Stuart, not Stewart. The finest tutors and instructors were provided—thirty-seven children of the nobility were brought up with the Dauphin and his sisters. Modern languages were important in a royal schoolroom, for Ysabel was now betrothed to the English King—Edward, whose father had been so determined to make the Queen of Scots his bride.

There was nothing amateurish or frivolous in the most polished court of Europe, where enjoyment was cultivated as an art. The children were taught to be skilled dancers, and Mary with two of her Maries took part in a classical ballet composed

Marie of Guise, 1558
By Corneille de Lyon
Scottish National Portrait Gallery, Edinburgh

IACOBVS.QVINTVS.SCOTTORVM.REX ❦ · MARIA.LOTHORINGIA.ILLIVS.IN.SECVNDIS.NVP

TVS.VXOR · ANNO·ÆTATIS·SVE·

by Catherine de Medici. So dark is the shadow in which the
French Queen stands that it obliterates her love and patronage of
art.

In the country homes of her Guise relations Mary joined a
carefree family circle. Her cousins, soldiers' exuberant sons, were
as zestful, as lively, as full of spirit as she was, and with them
she lived a healthful open-air life.

The country seat was the proud castle of Joinville, the motto
of whose town warned 'Beware when all things are safe.' Mary's
grandmother, Antoinette de Bourbon, was the centre of the
family. Her tender-hearted letters belie her tall proud looks. Not
only her own children but her daughters-in-law turned to her,
and all her grandchildren knew her watchful care. Her mind had
the stillness of depth that true religion imparts. This was the
high noontide of the Guise fortune, a mother surrounded by
sons strenuous with life; yet she was to out-live all except one,
a cloistered daughter, of her ten children.

Mary was with her grandmother and her Cardinal uncle when
she made her first communion at Easter 1554. She was devoutly
brought up in the Roman Catholic faith: her mother stipulated
she should attend Mass every day. It was from her religion that
she and her contemporaries learnt the discipline of obedience
to those in authority over them. No royal child would have
dreamed, far less dared, to question their parents' right to gov-
ern and order their lives. Mary was subject to her mother and
her uncles, particularly the Cardinal of Lorraine.

No detail of his niece's daily life was too small for the Primate
of France to overlook. He kept his sister in Scotland informed of
everything that happened to her, noting to the mother that
meanness was the thing her daughter abhorred most in the
world. He was always considerate to tell her of any ailments

Mary's Father and Mother
  Devonshire Collection,
  Hardwick Hall (National Trust)

once they were safely over, such as toothache or indigestion from eating too much melon. The strain of anxiety when the child really fell ill can be read between the lines of even his carefully reassuring letters.

Her twelfth year was an important one for Mary. Not only did she made her first communion, but she was allowed to have a separate establishment of her own, and her first guest was her Cardinal uncle, whom she entertained to supper. He took pains to explain she had now reached an age when she was capable of governing; but many thought he wished to withdraw her from the French Queen's influence. Madame Ysabel and Madame Claude were not permitted independent households. Instead, their mother made them sleep in a room within hers, so that they could do nothing but she knew of it, see no one without her cognisance.

Probably there was no one Mary loved so much as her mother. Through the formality of a very humble and very obedient daughter writing to Madame her mother, the confidence of that love breaks through. From her earliest days she was eager to re-pay service, careful as she was to be until the very end of her life for all the members of her household, writing to her parent about their advancement. She asked her mother to send over Shetland ponies she had promised to the Dauphin's brothers, wrote she was despatching to her one of the new watches that sounded the hours, and enquired about the embroidered sleeves for herself which were being worked in Scotland.

Early she learnt to keep state secrets, assuring her mother that nothing she was told would be known through her. We read that the bearer of their letters was sometimes Arthur Erskine—the faithful Arthur Erskine who years later was to have the horses ready for Mary to escape from Holyrood in the howe-dumb-dead of the night. The daughter, on the advice of her Cardinal uncle, sent the mother, to use as she thought fit, blank sheets of paper signed by her Marie, some 'La bein votre Marie' and six 'Votre bonne sœur Marie'. She kept her mother advised of the audiences she granted and the addresses she received from the rival factions in Scotland, reported to her news of the Duke of Chatelherault, 'I am told his words are finer than his deeds', and informed her of the reply she had made to the Earl of Huntly's plea.

No note of criticism was heard in the chorus of praise that greeted the Scots Queen from the moment she set foot in France. She was adulated, extolled, loved and adored, called perfect. Yet she remained singularly free of vanity. Royalty was in her blood and she accepted the pre-eminence of royalty as she accepted her blood. She wore her birthright as to the manner born, without the necessity of affectation, formality or complacency.

Her portraits give us no true picture when we know the effect she had on those who met with her. For one thing, it was, at least for women, one of the ugliest periods of dress, which, heavy and costly, burdened its wearer like furniture or caparison. Only the beauty of Mary's hands, wearing a ring on her thumb, escapes from the weight of these jewelled, ruffed, laced, oversleeved garments. Her loveliness was a loveliness that no brush could catch, as it cannot trap the burnishing of a flame. With her gold-flecked eyes, her russet hair and grace of movement, her beauty depended not so much on feature as the play of feeling, an air, and colouring that had the warmth and glancing brightness of sunlight.

She was beginning to grow tall but she still had the immature figure and narrow shoulders of a girl when her wedding, never far from the Guises' thoughts, was discussed. The arrangements took time to complete between the Scots Estates and the French King, who had the comfortable conviction that all foreigners had been created for the convenience of the French. It was impossible for the Queen Regent to leave Scotland, but a commission of nine of the country's leading men in church and state was appointed to be sent to France to act on behalf of the realm in the final negotiations and to be present at the ceremony.

The betrothal of their niece to the King's eldest son was the greatest triumph the house of Guise had yet achieved. Never had they been so popular. The Duke had taken Calais from the English, who had thus lost their last possession in France. He was a national hero, their defender and deliverer. Of France's great soldiers throughout the centuries, Francis of Guise must be numbered as one of her greatest.

The marriage was made unpopular in Scotland because of the tax of £60,000 raised to defray expenses. Ill luck dogged the commission from the start. The voyage was of the stormiest, and two of their ships were lost, one containing all their wedding-garments and decorations. Somehow the nine Scots envoys seem apart, by themselves, never quite to belong, guests who looked on from outside the family circle. Scotland hardly came into this French picture. The bride had grown up amongst them and they had taken her to their heart: she was one of them, not a stranger from over the sea. Also, this was the first time for over two hundred years a Dauphin had been married at home. France was ready to make more than a day of this wedding.

The commission represented the church, the nobility and the burgesses of Scotland. For the church there were the Archbishop of Glasgow, the Bishop of Ross and the Bishop of Orkney. Fine old Scots family names appear among the others: Rothes and Cassillis, Fleming and Seton, Erskine of Dun, and Lord James Stewart, Prior of St. Andrews.

He had been Prior of one of the wealthiest monastic foundations in Scotland since the age of four. He was the eldest of her husband's chance-bairns whom Marie of Guise had found when she arrived in her new country. But for the fact that he was born on the wrong side of the blanket, he, and not her infant daughter, would have been crowned sovereign after their father's death.

The illegitimate son of a king, James Stewart had enough of the divine right within him always to put himself first. He had renounced, in favour of Protestantism, the Roman Catholic faith, but not the revenues of the rich priory of St. Andrews. This buttering of his bread on both sides was characteristic of him. He was twenty-six when he arrived in France to dance at his half-sister's wedding, an unmarried man of rectitude, calculating and able, and as purposeful as cold steel.

The commissioners were particular to protect Scotland's independence in the drawing up of the marriage-contract. They agreed that the Dauphin, once he was married to their Queen, should bear the title King of Scots, but they refused the French King's request that the Scots regalia be sent to France with which to crown his son. The Estates knew well that it would be easier to bear the honours of Scotland, hallowed with age and history, into than out of France. Hard-headed Scots, the commissioners looked after the bride's pecuniary interests in case of her widowhood, a likely enough eventuality when the delicacy of the bridegroom was taken into account. It was because of their foresight that Mary was able to provide herself with any comfort in the dreetling years of her imprisonment.

What would the commissioners have felt had they known that shortly before her marriage, their young Queen signed three secret documents in which, in the event of her death without issue, she willed Scotland to France?

The private papers were signed at the wish of the French King and on the advice of her uncles a few days before the ancient ceremony of handfasting took place. Obviously, from the second document, she was led to believe that her country's preservation was entirely due to France who had poured money into

Scotland during her father's lifetime as well as her own. France, of course, had done no such thing. Her Cardinal uncle had written some years earlier to his sister in Scotland about Mary having her own household, 'You must not hope for any help from this side, because the King says that the revenue of the realm is very small, and so he cannot support her (Mary). And if in future the King grants a subsidy for the fortifications in Scotland, he will have to make corresponding deductions from her expenses here in France.' Not one French soldier would have been sent across the sea had it not served France's purpose to send him.

Mary has been blamed for selling her country, but she dearly loved giving and was probably proud she had something to bestow to discharge an apparently illimitable debt. Besides, on the eve of marriage, little more than fifteen, she would not be thinking of dying without issue. She would be thinking of living. She, who had been Queen of Scotland all her life, would be Queen of France one day, and it was France that really mattered. Scotland was remote and taken for granted as the past or background to her; France immediate as the present, potential with the future.

Paris was glad with spring on the wedding-day. The citizens had hung tapestries from their windows and garlands across the crowd-fevered streets. Gold and silver, heaped in baskets, were waiting to be thrown to the masses. A huge pavilion, where the actual marriage was to take place, had been erected outside the Cathedral of Notre Dame, and the Duke of Guise, as Grand Master, made himself popular with the people moving the lords on the dais that the crowds could have an uninterrupted view.

Excitement thrilled along the waiting onlookers in waves as the processions passed on their way to the Cathedral. Mules bore the city fathers in their crimson and yellow robes; the air of the city palpitated with the marching feet of the archers, the armed town-guard, and the lusty Swiss halberdiers with their band. Bishops, cardinals and abbots passed, followed by chanting choirboys whose lighted tapers flared in the draught. Gaily clad minstrels drifted by to the music of the pipe, windy flute and reverberating tabor. The Scots minstrels came, clad in the royal red and yellow, flinging their wild notes on the air.

The Dauphin, led by his uncle and followed by his three brothers, walked under the arches to the pavilion. A little over fourteen, he must have appeared very small. The wedding has been well chronicled but no description is given of the bridegroom. No one had eyes for anyone but the bride.

Heralded by a fanfare of trumpets and led by the King, she progressed slowly towards the pavilion. She wore a crown, a white robe with intricate decorations and elaborate adornments, a rich mantle and a velvet smoke-coloured train which was so long and heavy with jewels it took nearly a score of maids-of-honour to carry it.

The words of the marriage service were the same as those used for any ordinary couple. They were married in sight of all the people under the blue pavilion where the golden lily of France flowered on the silken roof. It was the lily that was conspicuous that day, not the assertive Scots lion on the bride's arms, but there was an old saying that was to be carved on one of her jewels, 'Fall what may befall, the Lion will be lord of all.'

Holding hands, the Dauphin and Dauphiness of France passed through the shadowed doorway of the Cathedral to hear High Mass, leaving outside the hot heaving crowds scrambling and fighting for the largesse thrown to them by the heralds.

Presented with beautiful gifts, the Scots commissioners at last took their leave. They were informed the £60,000 raised for the marriage expenses was not sufficient and a further £150,000 must be found. At Dieppe all nine were violently ill, and four of them died. The cry of poison at once went up, but it was a sickly

season and the malady probably a seaport epidemic. James, the
Queen's half-brother, recovered because of his youth and good
constitution, but he was said to suffer from the ill effects for the
rest of his life. It certainly was a case of the survival of the
fittest as far as he was concerned, for we are told he was 'hanged
by the heels by the mediciners, to cause the poison to drop out.'

Changes were taking place that were separating and altering
inevitably the whole course of the lives of the royal children
who had been brought up together, conned lessons and danced
with one another. Madame Ysabel would never become Queen
of England now, for the king to whom she had been betrothed
was dead. When peace was arranged between the old enemies
France and Spain, she, as France's earnest-penny, was betrothed
as his third wife to Philip II of Spain. This grim dark livid man,
more than twice her age, was quite a different bridegroom from
the princely fair-skinned English boy.

Her younger sister, the twelve-year-old Claude, found herself
with a more prepossessing husband—the youthful Duke of Lorraine. Brought up at court, he had all the attractive qualities
such an education could instil allied to a kind and generous
nature and the Guise good looks.

Thousands of crowns were squandered on the lavishness of
their wedding celebrations. The King and princes taking part in
the festal jousting were clad in cloth of gold and silver at the
expense of the young bridegroom, who presented fur-lined robes
to the lords and ladies of the court, including his cousin Mary
Stewart.

This marriage was to give Catherine de Medici her only grand-
son. It was a further triumph for the ever-soaring house of Guise-
Lorraine. In the acclamation and pride of the moment no one
thought to remember the old motto at home, 'Beware when all
things are safe.'

CHAPTER FOUR

The King of France came down the hill,
And ne'er went up again.

MARY was happy in her marriage. The Dauphin's health had
always been precarious, and this delicacy called out all
that was loving and compassionate in her. She paid deference
to her youthful husband but it was noticed when they granted
audiences, she took upon herself to do most of the speaking.
This tacit arrangement suited both, for Francis was not inter-
ested in councils and envoys. Indoors he had the petulance of
the bored. It was out of doors that he became feverishly alive,
playing tennis or leading the chase.

While Mary had been growing in France, the Protestant party
had been growing in Scotland; while she was attending High
Mass in the great cathedrals of Paris, Chartres, Rheims and
Rouen, they were breaking images, destroying cloisters, putting
monks to flight.

Burnings there were in her northern kingdom when the Catholics were in power, but no massacre of St. Bartholomew, no holo-
caust as in England, are found at Scotland's door. That Marie
of Guise was not a Catherine de Medici or a Bloody Mary Tudor
is not the whole explanation. The Reformation came late to
Scotland and found a productive soil in the common people.
It had not the slow growth that it had in France. The infallibility of a Church was replaced by the infallibility of a Book,
which gave the people that grandeur of the spirit that asked only
for the essentials. No longer content with pasturage in outworn

unfallowed fields of thought and usage, they turned to a faith which dared to break up the ground. There they came across not new seed, but the seed that had been planted when twelve men followed their Master through the fields of Galilee and stony Judaea. The Roman Catholic Church lost ground in Scotland because it had first lost its hold on the people.

It carried within itself the seeds of its own dissolution, for not one of its sons was to go to the stake for celebrating Catholic rites when the Protestants were strong enough to forbid them. And the Protestants were gathering their strength for that time.

Like the men of war who encompassed Jericho, John Knox, a host in himself, was metaphorically encircling the doomed Church with the trumpet-blast of his rallying-cries, volleys and war-notes. The people identified themselves with him, this man active with vehemence, his heat to redress wrongs, his capacity for hate. He was their voice, he spoke for them; and they were purged listening to the thunders, judgments and warnings that issued from his mouth. Despite the violence of his invective, the preacher was not as bloodthirsty as he sounded, neither were those who listened to him. There were cracked crowns and rough laughter, but no lynchings.

A Scot shares with the German Luther and the Frenchman Calvin the Reformation stage. To us, Knox always steals the thunder; even at this distance in time, he is more than lifesize. But his contemporaries saw not the part he played, but the man who filled it, an insignificant man looked at from certain quarters. When he wrote to Marie of Guise asking her for liberation and reform, she dismissed his letter with an inconsequential jest.

These early months of marriage were disturbed for Mary by letters from her mother. Forced against her will by French commissions to assert the ancient religion, she was deserted by the Scots nobles: leading them was Mary's half-brother, James Stewart. In vain Mary wrote to her mother, 'I hope you will be the means of restoring them to God and their duty.' Perth was the first city to throw off the Holy Faith; St. Andrews followed. The beautiful cathedral, monasteries and other sacred buildings were looted and destroyed. A fanatic preacher, John Knox, was inciting the people to rebellion—'Pull down the nests,' he told them, 'that the crows might not build again.' Images were paraded about the streets that the staring populace might see how they had been deceived believing it was a miracle when the Madonna bowed to them on certain feast days. Stirling was 'purified.' Edinburgh needed little inciting; the burghers were the firmest Protestants in the country and chose Knox to be their minister now they had done away with priest and bishop. The mob, out of hand, sacked not only the abbey but her palace of Scone. Every far-awa-screed from her mother added to the anxiety not only for her safety but for the safety of her daughter's kingdom, and the strain of bad news acted on Mary physically. Once in church she would have fainted but for wine brought from the altar.

Thrones were the nerve centres of that world, and events such as death or consecration that affected one of these seats of nature was felt in varying degrees by all. When Mary Tudor of England died, heart-broken at the loss of Calais, her half-sister Elizabeth was crowned in her place. But since their religion did not countenance divorce, Elizabeth was illegitimate in Roman Catholic eyes and Mary Stewart, grandchild of Henry VIII's sister, the rightful heir to the English throne.

The French King therefore claimed that his daughter-in-law was Queen of England, and the English royal arms were engraved on her seal and plate, embroidered on her tapestry, and emblazoned on her carriages. There they were a constant source of irritation and resentment to the English ambassadors, whose spite about their youthful bearer sounded the first note of discord in the paeans of praise that had accompanied her sojourn in France. 'The Queen of Scots is very sick,' wrote one; 'God take her to Him as soon as may please Him.'

It was when Paris was jubilant with celebrations that public assertion of Mary's right to the English throne was made. The gaieties were in honour of her companion Ysabel's marriage by proxy to Philip of Spain, a marriage that was expected to seal eternal peace between two old enemies. The lengthy elaborate festivities and ceremonies lasted for days and nights. At the great tournament heralds preceded the car of the Scots Queen crying out, 'Place! Place! pour la Reine d'Angleterre!'

She sat in the tribune watching her father-in-law, a master in feats of arms, break a lance with the Duke of Savoy and another with her favourite uncle, the Duke of Guise. Thunderous applause greeted the victories of the King, who wore the black and white of his favourite Valentinois.

The tournament was almost over when he suddenly challenged the young captain of the Scots Guard to contest with him. The Count of Montgomery would have liked well to decline the honour but his royal opponent insisted, and the trumpet sounded again. Mary saw her father-in-law shudder in his saddle at the impact as the contestants met.

A tremor went through the royal tribune. People were turning their heads and listening, but it was not at the King they looked. Catherine de Medici had half-risen in her seat, visibly agitated. She had been troubled with dreams and forebodings and wished the jousting to cease. She sent a message to the King, imploring him not to run another course, but he laughingly said he would ride only once more. He was anxious to try the war horse, 'Le Malheureux', the Duke of Savoy had given him and he was chagrined at having to give way, before his foreign guests and the ladies of the court, to so young a man as the Count of Montgomery.

At the first shock of the second encounter, the lances of both

men were broken. The captain's carried away his opponent's
visor; the broken lance could not be lowered quickly enough, and
the shaft glanced from the steel breastplate and buried itself in
the King's temple.

Women screamed with terror, Catherine de Medici and the
Dauphin fainted, the weeping Duchess de Valentinois made an
effort to reach her lover but her limbs would not carry her. As he
was borne from the field, onlookers noted that the King lay very
still. The blue-lipped Dauphin was carried behind him, still in a
faint.

The patient made gallant rallies, ordering that the festivities
should be continued, asking them to assure his young captain
that he knew it had all been an accident. But as the days passed,
it was realised that he was not only going to lose his eye but his
life. Mary saw her young husband stricken and frenzied, moving
from room to room in the palace, wringing his hands, beating
his head against walls, crying out, 'My God! my God! how can
I live if my father dies?'

The most joyous city in the world was turned into the most
fearful. Decorations and triumphal arches were torn down; instead of balls, masquerades and ballets, there was weeping and
lamentation. The black of dool shrouded where garlands had
fluttered, bells that had rung out now tolled; at an unbearably
slow pace the funeral procession moved through the muffled
streets.

Perhaps the first time Mary realised the significance of what
had happened was when she waited to allow her husband's
mother precede her as usual. The elder woman, as though suddenly remembering, drew back, and with a gesture half dreary,
half sorrowful, motioned her to go first. She, not Catherine de
Medici, was now Queen of France.

No longer had her kinsmen a vigorous forty-year-old King between them and absolute power. Now they had absolute power.

The sickly boy who had taken his father's place had no desire to be troubled with matters which interfered with his hunting and games. He told the deputation from parliament, sent to congratulate him on his accession, that he had assigned to his uncles of Guise the management of affairs. It was called the Reign of the Three Kings in France.

Her son paid Catherine de Medici exaggerated honour, as if to placate her for the little influence she had. Mary and her uncles also rendered her every conceivable outward respect, but that massive figure blocking out the light was not deceived. The English ambassador wrote to his sovereign, 'The Queen of Scotland is a great doer here and takes all upon her.' Her uncles excused every unpopular move they desired to make with the formula, 'The King wills it so, because his mother desires it.'

In a storm of rain and wind Francis on a white horse rode into Rheims, the holiest city in France, for his coronation. Because of the recent death of his father, the court was ordered to wear mourning, and gold, jewellery and embroidery were forbidden. One alone the decree did not touch. The black cloud of witnesses acted like a background to his young wife, shining with jewels and richly dressed. She watched his coronation, did not share it with him, because she had already been consecrated queen at an unremembered ceremony in a draughty grey Scots town.

The King of Spain was asking for his child-bride. She was not yet fifteen, and Ysabel's immediate departure had been held up because Paris had not yet completed her most important dresses. But at last the day arrived when she had to set forth, a winter's day white with snow. She cried bitterly and piteously at parting, kissed her brothers and sisters over and over again, pled with her playfellow Mary never to forget her, and had to be led to the waiting litter.

The sun gleamed and dazzled on frozen plains and the frosted trees stood out, white, ethereal and still, like the trees in a tapestry. Ysabel had no more tears to fall. As she looked out hungrily at the buildings which threw blue shadows on the snow-covered landscape, she cried, 'O, are there houses and castles as beautiful as these in Spain?'

The inspiration that so often inaugurates a new reign, the release of something no longer circumscribed by familiar horizons, the novelty of beginning, seem lacking in the time of Francis II's. Perhaps the practised hands that really held the strings robbed it of some of its impulse.

No longer could Francis be called 'le petit roi,' for he was taller now than his tall young wife. Since his coronation he had grown with a startling rapidity, which gave him an attenuated over-shot appearance, but such rapid growth was not healthy.

Letters from her mother in Scotland, first troubled, were now desperate, and her health had begun to fail. Mary wrote as comfortingly as she knew how, telling her that the King would send succour—'which he has promised me to do, and I will not allow him to forget it.' Reinforcements sailed from Dieppe but four vessels foundered, a thousand infantry perished and the remainder of the flotilla had to put back to port. Francis himself wrote to his mother-in-law, saying he would not be happy until he heard a better report of her health and telling her if she returned to France she would not find better physicians than her daughter and himself. But such safe harbourage was out of the question for the Queen-Mother, whom the nobles deposed as Regent and besieged in Leith.

The Lords of the Congregation appealed to Protestant England for help against Catholic enemies, and Queen Elizabeth secretly sent four thousand pounds to aid the Scottish nobles. A roar of laughter or a volley of curses always accompanied the mention of Elizabeth's subsidy, depending on which side the speaker happened to be, for her bounty never reached the Congregation. It was snatched on its way by the Earl of Bothwell.

One of the Queen-Mother's difficulties in a country that was not her own was to know who was for and who was against her: as her bewildered French commander was heard to remark, 'He that is with us in the morning is on the other side in the evening.' But one Scotsman she could depend upon, although he was Protestant, and that was her lieutenant of the Border and Admiral of Scotland, the Earl of Bothwell.

To be King and Queen of France was quite different from being Dauphin and Dauphiness. 'We are seeing things here we never thought to see and are not more happy in our traitors and rebels than you are there,' Mary wrote from Amboise to her mother in Scotland. Religion was the politics of the times, and whoever did not subscribe to the established faith were traitors, heretics and rebels in the eyes of the rulers.

In France Protestants were not called Reformers or Lords of the Congregation, they were known as Huguenots. At the time of Mary's marriage they were estimated at between 300,000 and 400,000: protest emboldened by such numbers spelt revolt and called for instant suppression.

'But thank God!' Mary continued, 'they have been discovered and we have too many loyal subjects here to dread their menaces. I promise you it is quite time we bethought ourselves.' A conspiracy against the King's life was suspected but the Guise brothers must have been aware they were the chief marks at which any conspiracy aimed.

A few days after Mary wrote her letter what was known as the Tumult of Amboise was ruthlessly put down by the Guises, with Catherine de Medici making herself small in the background. From a window in the strongly fortified castle, the King, with his brothers and the ladies of the court, watched how his Protestant rebels met their death. The most reliable authorities do not mention Mary Stewart as amongst the sightseers.

We do know that only one had tears for the sights she saw that day, and that was beautiful Anne d'Este, wife of the Duke of Guise.

Restlessly the young couple moved from hunting-lodge to hunting-lodge: no one was allowed to know where the King would sleep to-morrow. He kept his brother-in-law, Charles of Lorraine, near him for company and Mary his wife and sister-in-law, the Princess Claude. They were all young; of the four not one had yet reached twenty, and a wistfulness clings to these summer days, as though they would fain keep what they could of the past in the face of an altering world.

The death of her mother was concealed from Mary for ten days, but at last her Cardinal uncle broke it to her. As no one could comfort her when she heard of her parent's illness, so no one could comfort her now she knew of her death. Her grief was such that she passed from one agony to the other. With the death of Marie of Guise, something passed from her daughter's life never to return. Her mother loved her as no one else was to love her, a completely selfless love, unlike that of ambitious kinsmen to whom she was valuable or the men who were to court her.

Marie of Guise had taken refuge in Edinburgh Castle when she died, her lips cold before life left her. She lived her philosophy even on her death-bed, where she was reconciled to the lords: 'I pass over as gently as I can, preventing things from getting worse, waiting for a better time, and until I see what it may please God to appoint.' The better time for her was death before she was forty-five, which spared her seeing what it pleased the Lords of the Congregation to appoint.

A young Scotsman arrived at the French court at a time when the Scots were openly detested. His name was James Hepburn, fourth Earl of Bothwell. He had left Scotland before the death of his royal mistress to try to enlist help for her in Denmark and France, where they made him Gentilhomme de la Chambre. He was content enough to stay for the present, since Scotland was not large enough for him and his enemies and his loyalty had cost him his principal castle. But he had in his veins the strong restless blood of the Border, that ballad country lying between England and Scotland, and no Borderer was content to stay in one place for long.

The rumour that a royal child was expected circulated freely through the French court. The Guise desired it so ardently as a safeguard to their power that they made themselves believe it to be true; but Mary's condition, which gave rise to the report, was soon found to be nothing more than a temporary indisposition, and the delusion faded, leaving many triumphant and Mary sick at heart.

Within two months of the Queen-Mother's death, the Scots lords summoned, without the consent of their sovereign in France, a parliament which abolished the Pope's jurisdiction and established Protestantism as Scotland's religion. They sent a commission to France for their Majesties' confirmation of their acts, a one-man commission. To Queen Elizabeth they despatched an ambassade of three earls with their followers, thanking her for her assistance.

In Mary's day there was neither protocol nor etiquette shielding royalty in matters of state. As queen she could not depute; she came face to face with envoy, minister, courtier or statesman. Mary met the adroitest brains in this game of thrust and parry, and was to prove herself worthy of their mettle, with a charm that so often left them surprisingly unarmed.

She was not yet eighteen when she granted audience to the one-man commission from Scotland, Sir James Sandilands, who was not even an elder son, and who had been no friend to her mother. Young and spirited, touched on her royal prerogative, she betrayed a flash of the Stewart temper in her pronouncements.

He was told that to send him by post to his queen, and a great embassy with seventy horses to Elizabeth was discourteous. She refused to sanction any of the acts of a parliament which had assembled without her authority. Those who sent him must be taught that their duty was to assemble in their sovereign's name, not in their own, as though they would make Scotland a republic. They who boasted about the laws of their realm kept none of them. She regretted that the King her husband was not well enough to admit him into his presence, but informed him that he coincided in all her sentiments.

Francis had returned from the hunt, as he always returned, in an over-stimulated, exhausted condition, but that night he seemed more fevered than usual and it was feared he had caught a chill. He declared nothing could quench his thirst and complained of pains in his head and noises in his ear. He was so indisposed the following day that he did not leave Orleans as had been arranged.

His illness increased, to the terror of the Guises, who knew their day of power was over the moment life left the King's body. And to their despairing eyes it seemed as though that were going to happen. The historian pointed out that male Medicis seldom reached middle age, the astrologer told from the sky that only the briefest of lives was ordained for him, and the physicians read the same tale in his feeble frame.

The fearful Cardinal of Lorraine tried to will death away by the machinery of his calling, prayers, invocations to the saints, processions, masses and expiatory ceremonies; while the Duke of Guise strode up and down the antechamber, alternately accusing and threatening the physicians who were unable to save one in the flower of his youth.

In the close-shrouded sick-room the banked-back hostility felt for Mary Stewart by Catherine de Medici smouldered into bitter dispute. It was to his wife, who never left him, her son turned, upon her he had leant; she was his angel. The wife had therefore alienated the son from the mother.

He was beyond both wife and mother now, nothing coming from him but a soft, hollow rattling sound. There were those who said the mother was not sorry to see him, who was more Guise than Valois or Medici, breathe his last. The wise Venetian ambassador foresaw that everyone would forget the young King except the wife who had loved him.

The Reign of the Three Kings was over.

CHAPTER FIVE

Misty-moisty was the morn,
Chilly was the weather.

Hardly had Francis died than Mary was made to realise the difference between reigning Queen and Queen-Dowager of France. The Crown Jewels were demanded from her and taken possession of by the Regent, Catherine de Medici. The Cardinal of Lorraine had to relinquish on the same day the seal of Francis II, which was broken in the presence of the new King and his mother. Catherine de Medici now slept in the room of her ten-year-old son, so fearful was she that a Guise might step between them.

It did not take her long to rid herself of the Cardinal, and no one at court was sorry to see him go, for he could be both proud and over-bearing. Nor had power endeared him to the people, who had hanged his effigy in Paris. The Duke of Guise still lingered on, always followed at a distance by twenty of his swarthy Italian henchmen who never let out of their sight the solitary figure of their master.

In family sorrow, as at the rejoicing of wedding or christening, the Guise grandmother was there. That spare figure, with the long, thin nose and eyes that pierced from a world-weary face, shared with her young granddaughter the forty days of her seclusion as a widow. During that time Mary saw no daylight and never left her heavily curtained apartments, hung with mourning. Dressed in white, she looked pale as a taper in the blackness of the room where her grandmother knelt in prayer.

Only once did she emerge from her suffocatingly close sur-
roundings and that was to attend her husband's funeral service.
One of the Scots nobles present was to remember the enormous
black hood she wore that day. It was a solemn ceremony of dirge,
aspersion and procession, but no undue pomp for one who had
been King of France and King of Scotland. When his body was
removed for interment, it was taken by night and few attended
it on its last journey. Francis had ceased to be of importance or
interest to anyone but his wife when he lay on his twitching
death-bed; she alone wept for him now he was gone. The French
people knew that, and their love went out to the lonely Reine
Blanche, their hate to her uncles who had served not their king
but themselves and could forsake his dead body. The old taunt
that the Guises were Lorrainers and not true Frenchmen was
found scrawled on a piece of paper attached to the velvet pall
covering the King's coffin.

Mary's eighteenth birthday was spent in the dreariness of her
mourning-chamber, as was the passing of the old year in which
she had lost both mother and husband. In her sorrow she wrote
some sad sweet verses poignant with simplicity, with lines inevi-
table as epitaphs, 'My youth's bright morning flies,' 'My star of
hope is set,' 'My bliss is now my woe.' Because there was so
much that was happy and to her good bound up in Francis's
death, she began to think of his departure from earth as the departure of an angel. The mourning medal she caused to have
engraved bore the words 'Earth hides my sweetness.' The un-
certainty of life, the irrevocability of death, filled her young mind
with melancholy which was bound up with racing time. She had
a watch made in the shape of a coffin, and another in the form
of a helmeted death's head.

The new King, who had for her a child's adoration, visited
her with his small brothers. She loved children, and her roots
were entwined in this family of her dead husband's as though

it were her own. Her watchful mother-in-law saw her often; the relationship between them on the surface was now one of commiserating cordiality. Later foreign ambassadors, to offer the condolences of their sovereigns, were admitted into the young Queen's presence where the few tips of candle-flames served to accentuate the gloom. All, even the English Throckmorton, spoke of the sincerity of her sorrow, of the becoming dignity and submissiveness of her demeanour. Only Catherine de Medici wrote with venom: 'She shows as much obsequiousness to me as she ever did.'

But the loss of her husband did not affect Mary so deeply as had the loss of her mother. She had not leant on Francis, but he on her; while the thought of her mother, despite the distance separating them, had given her a sense of security and confidence. Her death had been to her daughter what the sudden unforeseen failure of the last light on shore is to a far-off ship.

So much lost in so brief a breath space. How futile had been her dreams, and how long ago since she had thought of them as realities, when she had fired herself with the vision of the triple crowns of France, Scotland and England. Now she was no longer reigning Queen of France and she had antagonised her cousin, the English Queen, by proclaiming herself sovereign of England and thus proclaiming also to the world the other woman's illegitimacy. She had nothing left but the uncertain crown of Scotland and a dormant claim to the English throne, which had been mounted by one with the not unnatural Tudor resolution to hold on to what she had grasped.

Mary as a widow was not the same woman as she had been when a girl wife. It was not so much that she had changed: it was as though the days of her seclusion acted as darkness in which was developed, like a photographic plate, what was already there. As she emerged from what was an intensely personal experience, she bore on her the impress of the woman she was to become.

In the past she had always had strong men around her, her father-in-law and her uncles, men to whom she was accustomed to defer, whose will she made hers. Now she had nobody: her father-in-law was dead, and to her uncles, the soldier and clerical statesman, she was no longer of supreme importance. This solitariness she was to experience to the end of her life. Her frankness was a measure of her loneliness.

She found when she had no one upon whom to depend that she had a strong fearless will of her own to serve her. But the woman in her, and Mary Stewart was very much a woman, unconsciously sought for one stronger to whom she could submit. In this she was unlike her cousin Elizabeth who was more male than female. Even Mary's ambition, and she had the Guise ambition, was feminine. It was England identified with herself as sovereign that mattered to Elizabeth; it was being queen that mattered to Mary.

The scene begins to be set for this real-life play, the characters to take their places. Instead of Press reports, we have for coverage the despatches, letters and memorandums written by ambassador and minister, and no modern reporter had a keener news sense or a more avid ear for gossip than a Melville, a Throckmorton, Randolph or Sadler. The secret service of to-day has little it could teach that employed in England in Elizabeth's time. And at the heart of the network, like a spider waiting at the hub of the web it has spun itself, was a little man with a domed head—Cecil, her Secretary of State.

He had informers in every court, spies watching every foreign port, his private dossier of the Scots nobles who could be bribed —a long list, and few were the names that were not on it. His policy was simple for the intricate system he controlled: England must be kept Protestant. That explained his enmity of

Mary: her very existence now she was at large as a widow caused
warning tremors to reach him from wherever she was. The English ambassadors, who treated with her directly, fed him with
their reports. Their relationship with the Scots Queen had something of that curious relationship, akin to intimacy, that exists
between the spier and the spied on, the stalker and the stalked,
the hunter and his prey.

Throckmorton had busily speculated before her husband had
died whom the widow Queen would marry. Already suitors were
bidding for her hand. She would have been content to wait in
this flowery land for her husband's brother Charles and become
again reigning Queen of France, but between her and this desire stood a purposeful woman with a glooming stout face.

Mary's position was her predicament; every move she made
was bound to upset not only individuals but countries, and thus
create tension and crisis. Her potentialities as a widow were much
more alarming to Elizabeth and England than when she was
married to the King of France. Now she was a perpetual threat
to the *status quo*.

No longer was Elizabeth the jewel of jewels on the marriage
market: she saw her suitor kings abandon her to court the
younger Queen of Scots. If Mary married any of them, and the
King of Denmark was boasting he was the strongest prince upon
the sea, then strengthened by his power she could contest the
crown of England. But the alliance most dreaded by England
as well as France was a Spanish alliance, for that would give
Spain, already the first world power, a perilous preponderance.

Throckmorton wrote home that many reasons were put forward why the Queen of Scots should leave her close seclusion at
court: change of air for one thing, change of scene for another.
But he gave it as his opinion it was because negotiations for her
marriage could not be carried out when she was under the hourly
supervision of the Queen-Mother. He regretted her departure

as neither he nor his informers could follow her into the enclosed circle of her own family.

Her uncle, retired to his own bishopric, was scheming his utmost to bring about the marriage of his niece with Don Carlos, the stepson of her one-time playfellow Ysabel. He was two years younger than Mary, a sickly unattractive boy, but, as heir to the mighty far-flung monarchy of Spain, he was the most sought after bridegroom in Christendom.

Queen of Spain, Queen of Scotland and, if God grant her years, who knew but Queen of England. It was a high-pitched but momentous refrain to which to tune a life.

In those early days of wistful spring the negotiations for the marriage proceeded as well as any Guise could wish. But while the confidential Cardinal was treating with King and ambassador, a woman could be seen bending over her letters, writing to her daughter in distant Spain. She wrote complaining bitterly of one known well to them both, a woman whom she disguised under the name of 'the gentleman' lest her letters fell into the wrong hands. Emphatically she told Ysabel that she knew very well her stepson must marry no one but her little sister Marguerite.

Mary's spirits, ever resilient, began to revive as she moved amongst those who loved her. She broke her journey at Paris to inspect her robes and jewels, on her way to Rheims where she was received by four of her uncles. In the holy city she stayed with her Cardinal uncle and spent Easter attending the daily services. From Rheims she travelled by easy stages to the family home at Joinville. The glorious landscape she knew and loved unrolled before her eyes, where the air was radiant as a halo and vibrant as a harp-string, and colour changed every moment on pasture, rock, river and orchard, as though light were a tide passing over the earth.

As she journeyed through the fertile countryside of France,

two men were making towards her from Scotland. One was her half-brother, James Stewart, spokesman for the Protestant lords; the other, despatched at the same time, a representative from the Catholic party. The Catholic beat the Protestant, for John Lesley reached his royal mistress a day before James Stewart.

A cleric of the Roman Catholic Church, Lesley was one of its most dexterous champions. He was in his mid-thirties when he arrived post-haste at Vitry-le-François, but already he looked venerable because of his gravity, with hooked nose, a small beard and the high capacious forehead of the scholar.

He brought all the powers of his considerable diplomacy to bear on his young sovereign, warning her that his rival making all speed to reach her wanted her crown for his own head. He brought her the promise of faithful service and duty from all the principal nobility, bishops, clergy and burghers of the north of her country, entreating her to land with a French force at Aberdeen, where all were of her religion. There she would be met with 20,000 men led by the Earl of Huntly, a force strong enough to be able to repeal with a high hand all the statutes that had been passed by an illegal parliament, and to re-establish the old faith.

Mary did not need her uncles to advise her that if she returned to her realm, she must go as queen of all her people. She was a Stewart and the basic Stewart creed of kingship was the unity of Scotland. To return to her native land with civil war was repugnant to her, and she had only to apply her secret gauge to Huntly to find him wanting: shiftless and unreliable, he had been disloyal to her mother.

The earnest man before her measured up to her test, and she kept him beside her. But few, indeed none, came through it with the flying colours that the Earl of Bothwell did. His faithfulness had withstood the strain of finding himself on the losing side. Not that Bothwell would ever admit his side to be the losing one, so sure and prompt was his bearing. The English ambassador wondered what that vainglorious, rash and hazardous young man was up to when he left the French court, boasting he would live in Scotland despite all men.

Mary knew he would be loyal to her, as he had been loyal to her mother. But he did not fit into the scheme of things, he belonged neither to one party nor the other. A Protestant, he hated the English as much as they hated him. His was one of the very few names that did not appear on Cecil's private dossier of Scots corruptible material: against Mary's half-brother appeared six words, 'The Lord James would be gratified.' He was a side in himself, this Bothwell, making his Commando raids across the Border. Men looked askance at the swaggering, lady-loved adventurer and wondered where women found his charm, but women loved him without asking why. Masterful and confident, he won his way too easily with them, and he was one of those who valued a thing until he had it.

James Stewart arrived the day after John Lesley. Both brother and sister had their father's hair, but there the resemblance between them ended. Her transparent face was full of light and colour, his forceful and frowning with deliberation. He had none of her charm, or her desire to please. He dealt according to his nature—'rudely, homely and bluntly'.

The meeting between brother and sister was bound to be trying and agitating for both, and Mary must have been glad it took place whilst she was amongst her French relations. There was something formidable about this Scots half-brother who had abandoned and fought against her mother and the old faith, and was known to be *persona grata* with Elizabeth, so acrimoniously hostile to Mary. On his part, he must have been well aware of his own powers, for he was the strong ruler his country needed, but he bore the bastard's bar and knew the crown belonged to his younger sister who was more French than Scots.

Gossip said a cardinal's hat was dangled in front of him at
Joinville if he would renounce the new religion, but this seems
improbable unless the Guises were counting on his cupidity. His
acquisitiveness fed on what it gathered in. The illegitimate son
of a king, possessions in his eyes were prerogatives, particularly
when possessions spelt land. But if the cardinal's hat were offered him, we have no reason to suspect that his refusal was anything but genuine. The very austerity of the new faith appealed
to something in his unbending nature; his home was known to be
more like a church than a court; and after John Knox he was the
most potent single instrument to establish the reformed religion
in Scotland.

He had come 'to grope' his sister's mind about her return to
her realm. Both he and those for whom he spoke were suspicious
of her uncles, lest they should try to use her to reassert a religion
now hateful to her countrymen. But he found Mary did not
press for the old alliance between Scotland and France to be renewed. It must be remembered that while she was seeing her
brother at Joinville, the negotiations for her Spanish marriage
were approaching a climax. She could not marry without the
consent of the Scots Estates, and that consent must have been
uppermost in her mind at that time.

She disliked the furtive fraternising with England that she
knew was going on to her detriment, but her brother was hopeful that an arrangement could be worked out beneficial to both
queens: in consideration of the surrender of Mary's claim to the
English throne, Elizabeth, if she had no heirs of her own, might
undertake to acknowledge Mary as her successor. Mary could
point out to James Stewart that she had given up bearing the
English arms since her husband's death, whereas the over-sensi-
tive Elizabeth insisted on quartering the French arms with her
own. When an irritated French ambassador pointed out to her
with Gallic logic the absurdity of styling herself Queen of France

since French law forbade a female to reign, she replied, 'Twelve sovereigns of England have borne the arms and style of France, and I will not resign them.' Unlike Elizabeth's claim to the French throne, Mary's successorship to the English was irrefutable: as her brother pointed out to the English sovereign his sister was 'next in lawful descent of the right line of Henry VII.'

Mary said good-bye to her brother and made her way, accompanied by her uncles, to Nancy. There she was welcomed by the youthful couple, Henri of Lorraine and the Princess Claude, who had been her childhood companions. They did everything with indoor and outdoor entertainments to restore the spirits of their guest, in an effort to bring back happier days, but it was at Nancy that the blow fell.

The Cardinal of Lorraine heard from Spain that there was no one whom His Catholic Majesty would more gladly match with his son than the Queen of Scots, but such a marriage could not be contemplated whilst the affairs of the Queen's Grace were on so insecure a footing.

At the same time a mother received a letter from a dutiful daughter telling her that arrangements for a marriage between Don Carlos and Mary Stewart would proceed no further. Catherine de Medici knew well when she heard the Cardinal's niece was so ill of an ague she could not attend the coronation of little Charles that it was no ordinary fever which kept the girl abed.

There was nothing left for Mary but to return to her realm. Only when she was safely settled on her throne, wielding her sceptre over a submissive people, would the Spanish alliance become possible. She wrote that she hoped to live amongst her subjects in all content and amity, but content and amity were precisely what Elizabeth would do everything in her power to prevent her from having if and when Mary returned to the country across the Border. On the other hand, Catherine de Medici rejoiced to be rid of her inopportune daughter-in-law and sped

her on her way with every honour. Mary's uncles also urged her
to return to her native land: because of the Queen-Mother's hostility to her, their niece was now a hindrance to them instead of a
furtherance. They knew the Scots Roman Catholics were a
broken party, and advised her to 'serve the time' by accommodating herself to her subjects, taking her brother into her confidence and depending upon the strongest party, those of the
reformed religion.

At Joinville Mary bade farewell to her grandmother, and journeyed through the summer days to the coast where she was to
take ship. Every halting-place she said good-bye to someone, every hour looked back on scenes she would never see again. It
was like an uprooting, an untwining of tendrils from what she
had thought was part of herself. She joined the French court,
and passed from one royal palace to another, each with its memories of happiness that seemed to belong to another lifetime. In
the abbey where she had been reunited to her mother, she now
knelt to pray at that mother's bier.

She was conducted to the port by all her uncles, where she
parted with the Cardinal of Lorraine and her favourite, the Duke
of Guise, her eyes blind with tears. Three of her younger uncles
were to sail with her, and Scots and French ladies-in-waiting,
courtiers, poets and priests were in her train. The four Maries
who had accompanied her to France now returned home with
her: Mary Livingstone who was vigorous and called the Lusty,
Mary Beaton the prettiest, the brilliant Mary Fleming, and the
Queen's favourite, Mary Seton, the only one who was not to
marry.

As the ship sailed out of Calais, a profound mournfulness
stole over Mary, as though she knew intuitively that no longer
would those on shore build their fortunes on her. She was in
that highly fraught mood that read portent into any happening.
When a ship in the harbour capsized and all were drowned be-

fore her horrified eyes, she exclaimed, 'Ah, my God! what augury is this?'

She reached Scotland in about half the time that it had taken her to voyage by the west seas to France. A thick wetting mist blotted the shore from view when she arrived early one Sunday morning and her ships hove out of the haar like a phantom fleet.

Thus she returned to Scotland, armed only with her courage. The three traditional allies of her royal race had been the Church, France and the common people. Now the kindly old alliance with France was of the past, the Church upon which her fathers had relied was beaten and bruised, and she, a Roman Catholic Queen, had come to rule over a stoutly Protestant people.

The young Francis
By François Clouet
Bibliothèque Nationale, Paris

Mary at Sixteen
Attributed to François Clouet
National Portrait Gallery, London

Lady believed to be Mary Beaton
By an Unknown Artist
Scottish National Portrait Gallery, Edinburgh

Le Deuil Blanc, Mary in Widow's Weeds
By François Clouet
Scottish National Portrait Gallery, Edinburgh

BOOK TWO

Summer

August 1561 – June 1566

CHAPTER ONE

When I came to Scotland my heart it grew cold,
To see a little nation so stout and so bold.

THE star under which Mary Stewart was born was baleful: again and again she was to suffer from what can only be described as ill luck. And she had to endure not only the unexpected blows of misdirected fortune, but was caught in a tide of adverse circumstances beyond her control.

There is no need to wonder at how well she managed during those first few years on her return to Scotland. She came of a long line accustomed to rule, and faced crisis with presence of mind, always with courage and often with resource. Also she inherited her mother's magnificent vitality that not only adapted her to circumstances but gave her pleasure to do so.

It has truly been said that Elizabeth had all the right men round her, Mary all the wrong. The Scots nobility waiting to greet their Queen were on the whole a despicable band of men, each for his own house, and there was little to choose between those of the old religion and those of the new. The adherence of many of the Protestant lords to the new was often more a matter of profit than of religion. Certainly there were sterling men whose ardour for the Reformed faith was based on principle not policy, but they for the most part belonged to the lesser nobility. Amongst the higher, both Catholic and Protestant, scarcely one name rings true: every man had his price. The Scots nobility were of course too numerous for the country, and each to enlarge his own power had to grasp from someone else. Mary's kingdom was poor and bare, trampled bracken bush and lawless castle, or towns huddled with buildings down whose steep streets the wind cannonaded.

Her people's slumbering loyalty to their ancient line of kings was stirred and rekindled when they saw her and heard of her return. She had come home to them, her subjects, stepping on to her native soil accompanied only by attendants. No French soldiers to swagger here and there as though they had trysted the country. News of her arrival sped swiftly through the land, and her brother rode post-haste to welcome her.

As Holyrood was not yet prepared for her residence, Mary lodged the day of her arrival with a trader, who had known and been a faithful subject to her mother. Leith had meant much to Marie of Guise. There her daughter, brought up in all the glory and grandeur of France, waited with her French uncles and her train around her. She was in her own country, where men spoke more with their throats than with their mouths, and where in each house the poker and tongs were chained to the fireplace lest they be used as weapons when sudden quarrels arose.

The mist dispersed towards the afternoon, and Leith with its red roofs began to piece itself together. Her brother found her no whit daunted by the unpreparedness of her arrival: she could always be counted on to make the best of everything. It was not his fault that nothing was in readiness for her, for she had left France much earlier than expected, to mislead the English. Of the fleet of tall ships accompanying her on the voyage, three had fallen into their hands, two transporting the royal horses. Mary could have wished that some other of her vessels had taken their place when she saw the sorry hacks brought to carry her and her train to Edinburgh.

She set out at evening for Holyrood and arrived when night was beginning to fall—night that was pierced by hastily lit fires blazing on every near hill-top to honour the Queen's home-coming. It was a gallant day for Scotland now her sovereign had come home.

The long palace looked smaller than it really was, for it was low-lying and robbed of loftiness by the hills banked so closely behind it, as though to ward off any chance of escape. It had been ruthlessly sacked, even its library looted, by the English during the Rough Wooing of Mary's childhood, and her mother had made little attempt to restore it, probably through lack of money. After the soaring spaciousness of the French palaces to which she was accustomed, Mary's Scots homes must have struck her as secretive and closed in upon themselves.

To ears tuned to French perfection the music that greeted her in welcome was rude and discordant. A Frenchman in her train waxed heated about the vile fiddles, the chanted psalms so badly sung that nothing could be worse—'what music and what repose for her first night!' But Mary sent out a message thanking the serenaders, who took her warm praise so much to heart that they returned to repeat their performance on several nights.

For the next few days the steep narrow town of Edinburgh shook and rattled with the ringing horse hooves of the nobles who streamed from every direction to pay allegiance to their sovereign princess. She welcomed them more than they did her, making each feel in turn that she had sailed all the way from France to receive him alone, so gracious was she—over-affable, asserted some cavillers from Fife.

At her formal entry into Edinburgh some days later, she was borne through the city under a pall of purple velvet up the Lang Gait to the castle where her mother had died. Cannons fired a salute and she was followed by a procession of burgesses, all clad in the same garish apparel, which wound after her through the irregular streets like some strange, many-eyed, fabled animal. There were faces at every sunken, projecting and dormer window, bodies crowding on the forestairs and wooden galleries of the houses, jostling and elbowing each other in the shadowed wynds, to see their Queen ride by. She was accompanied by her four Maries, and for the first time saw her capital city that lay with its clambering streets between a palace and a castle.

At the Butter Tron little children in a flower-decked cart sang her praises, like small flutes out of tune. The keys of the city were presented to her by a boy, dressed as an angel, who was unsteadily lowered from a painted gate, and who also bestowed on the Queen a purple Protestant Bible. The nudging people watched what she would do with it; whatever that was, it would be wrong in their eyes. She did the correct thing, handed it to the Captain of her Guard, who happened to be Arthur Erskine—a pestilent Papist in the eyes of the onlookers.

Some pageant was arranged to take place at the congested Salt Tron, for there seemed to be a dressed-up figure amongst the noisy gathering. The Queen's train paused to watch what had been staged in her honour. Someone raised the figure on his shoulder and all saw it was the effigy of a priest with grinning slit mouth and boneless hands propped weakly in an attitude of prayer.

Catholic Huntly, who bore the Sword beside the Queen, rode furiously at the rabble, dispersing them here and there, scattering the faggots of the fire they had prepared and terrifying them with his unreined precipitancy.

On the following evening Mary gave her first banquet in Holyrood, which caught for the occasion something of the splendour of her grandfather's reign, when the Scots court was at its most magnificent. Mary, with her rich French dowries, returned to her native country a wealthy woman, and her ships were still being unloaded at Leith. There was much for her nobles to stare at, for there was much that many of them were seeing for the first time: carpets from Turkey for instance, instead of rushes on the floor. Rough walls were hidden by splendid arras of cloth of gold and cloth of silver; costly hangings and furnishings of velvet and damask were fringed with gold and so richly embroidered they looked jewelled. There were oaken and marble tables, sofas and porcelain, cabinets and silver lamps, superb canopies, the mark of royalty, and gorgeous beds.

Master Knox, in his house in the Netherbow, had to digest the unpalatable fact that everyone was flocking to their Queen, anxious to seek her favour. The Protestants, he noted, were not the tardiest. Yet the very face of heaven at her arrival should have warned them that she would bring Scotland nothing but sorrow, darkness, dolour and impiety. But the godly chose to fly in the teeth of such manifest signs and portents and made the same haste to pay court to her as the ungodly. To Knox the godly were the Protestants, the ungodly Catholics.

He loved her brother James Stewart as a son, and it was at a son's defection he cried out when Stewart, 'the man whom all the godly did most reverence', grimly kept the door himself that first Sunday that his sister could hear mass in her private chapel. After all, he had undertaken, as delegate of the Lords of the Congregation when he saw her in France, that she would be able to worship privately after her own religion. He tried to excuse himself now by saying he was keeping the chapel door to prevent any Scotsman entering to attend mass, but no one, Knox least of all, was deceived. At Mary's court there was 'some enchantment whereby men were bewitched', even those whom the godly did most reverence.

But there was one man that enchantment could not touch, and that was John Knox. Mary sent for him soon after her return. Knox was forty-six at this time, and forty-six was old in these days. Already he had begun to achieve legendary proportions to his countrymen. It is the background of the Old Testament we always see behind Knox, for he spoke with all the authority of an Elijah, his preaching powerful with prophecy. He was not heard of until he was approaching thirty, and his was the zeal of the hardening old. The Spirit was like 'a great gale' in him. Those searching eyes that probed the verities saw neither the beauty nor youth of the girl before him but stripped her of the only royalty she understood. A later pamphleteer was to jingle: 'A Scot and Jesuit joined in hand first taught the world to say That subjects ought to bear command and Princes to obey.'

Mary began by taking the offensive, accusing him amongst other things of inciting her subjects against her mother and herself, and being the author of a book whose very title was seditious, 'A First Blast of the Trumpet against the Monstrous Regiment of Women.' Knox replied, 'Madame, if it may please your Majesty patiently to hear my simple answers.' His simple answers ran to great length and Mary certainly listened to him with courteous patience, inserting when she could single sentences of her own. 'In communicating with her,' Knox wrote to Cecil, 'I espied such craft as I have not found in such age.'

If Mary hoped to be able to reinstate the old faith in Scotland, and there are indications that she not unnaturally did, she must have realised soon after her return the futility of any such dream. The most she could work for was for those of her religion to enjoy the same freedom of worship as did their opponents. To us in the twentieth century that seems reasonable enough, but the climate of the sixteenth was not ripe for tolerance. Knox and his contemporaries knew there was no room for the two religions to live side by side, even if one had been cut down to near extinction. Lest it once more take hold, the ground had to be scorched.

Mary wisely dismissed most of her French followers soon after her arrival, and they were only too glad to leave what was to them a heathen country where even the Queen's priests were

attacked. Her Council consisted of twelve members, of whom
seven were Protestant and five Roman Catholic. Personal hatred
between the fellow councillors divided even co-religionists. Between the nobles were hereditary enmities and feudal quarrels
handed as a bloody heritage from father to son. Peace and conciliation were sometimes formally brought about by the Queen
or her Privy Council, but two parties neither Queen nor Privy
Council could ever join were the Earl of Bothwell and the Earl
of Arran, eldest son of the mighty house of Hamilton and heir-
presumptive to the Scottish throne. Both were councillors but
Bothwell, who had had his father's old lands in Teviotdale restored to him, was a man of action and more at home on the
Borders than in the Council Chamber.

Keeping this heterogeneous band together was the young
Queen, and she handled the anomalous situation in which she
found herself with discretion, verve and tact. Even Knox had to
concede the seemliness and gravity of her demeanour in the
Council Chamber, but because she could do no right in his sight
he made himself believe she was but playing a part.

That autumn the Queen progressed to the principal towns of
her realm with her ladies and many of her noblemen. Memories
must have surged upon her in Stirling when she felt the first
draught of Highland air as she rode up the Hie Gait. The world
had been a place to wonder and marvel at in those days of long
ago when they had lifted her on to a hassock to see what could
be seen from the castle windows as she listened for the Saint's
Bell to chime.

Now as she journeyed from castle to palace, ruins of monastery and cathedral met her gaze, not razed by ruthless invading
hosts, greedy for objects to rend their destruction on, but by her
own people. Moss grew where monks and priests had trod; birds
flew through broken arches and niches that no longer held stone

figures of haloed saint and praying cardinal; the wind tapped at fallen walls of chapter-house and frater.

The shouts of acclamation to greet her were mingled with threatening declamations against her religion. She who had been the darling of France, accustomed all her life to adulation and praise, needed all the brightness of her bravery to hide what she was feeling, for this people took her popularity with them for granted. She fainted in Perth and had to be lifted from her horse. Her priests were beaten in Stirling, and at St. Andrews high furious words passed between her elder half-brother James and the corpulent, unwieldly Huntly when the Catholic told the Protestant he would set up Mass in three shires if the Queen commanded. The Queen did not command: she was the only sovereign living at that time against whom no instance of persecution is recorded. She remained longest at St. Andrews where foaming breakers broke on tawny sands: it was to be the place where she was happiest in Scotland.

Her train proceeded to Edinburgh, back to Holyrood which her servants and maids-of-honour brightly lit for her, filled with music and dancing, and light happy voices. But the gloom of the palace was only thrust back for the time being, and shadows lay heaped in the farthest corners as though waiting their time to advance.

The Catholics murmured that the Protestants ruled all, but Mary had learnt that to be sovereign of the realm of Scotland entailed queenly concessions. Better to concede graciously than be boldly flouted by a people who claimed their own conscience was both Pope and King. She allowed herself therefore to be guided by her brother and the man she had made her Secretary of State, Maitland of Lethington. Randolph, the English ambassador, wrote to Cecil that she was patient to bear, and bore much. But neither her brother nor her Secretary, nor even the

English Randolph, suspected that behind her docility was a hidden capacity for pursuing her own ends.

Perhaps nothing dwindles the intervening centuries so much as wit, and Lethington is nearer to us than many a man born centuries later, his personality has not dated. He was totally unlike the other Scotsmen round Mary. A Protestant, he wore his religion lightly, and was not zealous like Knox or entrenched like James Stewart. Accomplished, with the subtlety of the courtier and the brilliance of the scholar, his urbanity was cosmopolitan. He loved his native country of Scotland, but his patriotism had nothing provincial about it. He was one of the first to realise that Scotland's prosperity lay through alliance with England. 'The mark I always shoot at', he wrote, 'is the union of England and Scotland in perpetual friendship.'

He had reason to dread his young mistress's return because he had joined her mother's enemies when he had been her Secretary of State, for his policy was union with England, not annexation by France. The dexterity with which he changed sides won him the nickname of Chameleon, and his realistic politics roused mistrust in the common people who called him Mitchell Wylie, their corruption of Machiavelli. Elizabeth described him as the finest wit of any in Scotland, but he knew Mary looked upon him as 'the best Englishman of them all', and he foreboded her return would bring wonderful tragedies in its wake.

But when Queen and diplomatist met, the past was forgotten. Lethington spoke Mary's language. Her brother was brusque and unceremonious, he tactful and smooth. Lord James was sparing of words and made great efforts to achieve small ends. The Secretary, whose colourful imagination knew no confines, was never at a loss for the ready word, and could adroitly adapt himself to any audience or situation. James Stewart was courageous and valiant in battle; Secretary Lethington's fingers more readily held quill than sword, his chief weapon was his nimble tongue. Lord

James took himself, as he took everything, gravely, and was too occupied with his own purposes to find time to trifle or quip; whereas the courtier's tall, thin figure was the spindle of every gathering. The one attribute both men had in common was their morality in a licentious age.

Soon after her return from France, Mary and the wary Secretary, with his keen narrow face like a polished bone, could be seen elaborating blandishing letters to her English cousin, pressing her to name the Scots Queen as her successor. The fondest dream of Lethington's life, to see the Scots and the English crowns united in one, could best be realised through his royal mistress who was indisputably next of kin to the English Queen and therefore in direct succession to the English crown. But Queen Elizabeth knew that to pronounce Mary as her heir-presumptive was tantamount to signing her own death-warrant, because of the inducement it would give English Catholics to hasten her from the throne to make room for her successor. She therefore deferred the issue with a chain of half-promises, impossible stipulations and loving suggestions she had no intention of implementing.

Secretary Lethington posted to and from England, delighting the matter-of-fact English Queen with his apt, flattering tongue, and urbanely attempting to lead her into a position she needed all her dexterity to circumvent. He tried to whip some ardour into the chilling English Secretary of State by picturing for him how grateful posterity would be to them, the secretaries of both kingdoms, if they succeeded in bringing peacefully together under the one crown the two countries so long at enmity. But Master Cecil remained unmoved at the prospect of such future glory and equally determined that a Catholic Queen should never reign in England.

Flagging spirits were quickened by music-filled evenings spent with masques and banquets. It was a young court, and a court

accustomed to gaiety and laughter. Bothwell and the Queen's
French uncle enlivened them with their high unchecked vagaries
and buffoonery, and her two younger half-brothers, John and
Robert, with their wild leaping horseplay. How much more need
to be gay here than in sunny France, to speed by the long dark
hours with revelry, frolic and sprightly love-making. John Stewart was in love with Bothwell's sister, Robert Stewart sighed for
that of the Earl of Cassilis, the four Maries attracted suitors as
flowers attract bees. But it was not only in young veins that the
sap of love rose high. James Stewart's long wooing of the Earl
Marischal's daughter looked as though it would come to fruition
in this heady air, and the middle-aged Secretary of State realised
he was a widower.

Whispers about the strange mummings and merry-makings
sped up the forestairs into every dark dwelling in the wynds and
closes, made the ruffianly weavers pause as they worked at their
looms in the Netherbow, penetrated to the burn-the-wind in his
dim, darklit forge, caused the prick-the-louse to ask what the
world was coming to as he sat, cross-legged, snipping, threading,
seaming. Had the sword-cutler heard that she sat up all night
playing with the Deil's Book and that men dressed up as women
and, more shameful still, women as men—ay, and she among
them—while they danced their wanton French dances? Lord
James, some said, looked on—he certainly ought to have known
better. Some nights ago her giddy French uncle and the Earl of
Bothwell—he'll end ere he mends—had disturbed—wheest, no
names, but everyone knew who was meant, a merchant's daughter in the town, my Lord A—'s mistress. The Earl had had to
leave the town for a time to avoid cumber, but the Papist uncle
was still there. Wherever there's a Frenchman, there's trouble.
What was good Master Knox thinking of it all? He was preaching
against it every Sunday in the Great Kirk. The Lord be praised
that there was still one man in broad Scotland who was not
afraid to give tongue to what he thought.

CHAPTER TWO

When I gaed to the castle yett, and tirled at the
pin,
They keepit the keys o' the castle, and wadna
let me in.

As a young man James Stewart had betrothed himself to Christian Stewart, Countess of Buchan in her own right, but he had not married her. Instead he shut her up in his mother's keeping in Lochleven Castle once he succeeded in gaining her guardianship and her estates. And there she still was when the 'long love' between him and Agnes Keith, daughter of the wealthy and powerful Earl Marischal, matured into marriage.

The Queen, who made much of the bride, created her brother Earl of Mar and gave the marriage banquet, a magnificent affair, at Holyrood. Dancing, fireworks, pageants and masking marked so joyous an occasion. 'The greatness of the banquet, and the vanity used thereat offended many godly', observed Knox who always spoke for himself, and the breach between him and James Stewart widened perceptibly.

Another marriage had taken place a month earlier, at Bothwell's favourite castle of Crichton, when his sister was married to John Stewart, half-brother of the Queen's. It was a fine castle with large rooms one above the other, wide fireplaces and tiled floors, and Bothwell, who had had to sell some lands lately for ready cash, certainly put his best Border foot foremost to give his sister a splendid send-off. We read of eighteen hundred wild does and roes cooked for the feast in the great stone kitchen. He was rewarded for his pains by hearing the Queen's French uncle declare he had never seen such a bridal—no, not even in France. The Queen graced the banquet with her presence, spending the night at the castle which stood in the undulating country of the Borders. Lord James accompanied her—the bridegroom after all made the occasion something of a family affair; besides reconciliation between him and Bothwell had been effected by the Queen on her return to Scotland.

This is a good time, when Bothwell is at his best as host, to have a long look at him. He was twenty-seven when he feasted the Queen's Grace at his sister's wedding, so his character and bearing have had time to consolidate. His crest carved above the doorway was a bridled horse's head and neck: his motto 'Keep Trest—Keep Faith'. He was stalwart in build, not over tall, the glint of red about his hair. He had a hard smallish head, small ears, broad face and blue eyes with the wariness of the fighter rather than the thinker. Already the line between nose and mouth was strongly defined. He was good-humoured, accepting the reverses of fate as a soldier accepts the fortunes of war, and he had all the magniloquence of the Borderer. Ready to undertake any enterprise however hazardous, he was more ready to put it into execution. He knew all the rules of the game played by his sword-arm and would have deemed it dishonourable to break any of them: but he had no head for politics, for the delaying tactics of a Lord James, or the subtleties of a Lethington, or the cat-and-mouse game that a Cecil could play with all a diplomatist's consummate skill.

Mary was neither the scarlet woman painted by her detractors, nor the saint her admirers have gilded her: in her case, her detractors and admirers have been evenly divided. But neither have had a good word to say for Bothwell. Only in contemporary times has he come belatedly into his own with Robert Gore-Brown's study of him.

His parents were divorced and he was brought up under the

evil tutorage of his great-uncle, a Bishop of Moray. He certainly was not the uncouth savage some have made him out. He was educated in Paris, and had what few of his Scots fellow nobles could boast, a library. His books, handsomely bound in calf and tooled with the Hepburn rose and lions, include arithmetic and geometry, the natural sciences, and military history and theory, which he read in French translations from the Latin. When his fellow peers signed their names to bonds and deeds, they did so in the scrawling clumsy old-fashioned Gothic. When Bothwell added his, he used a clear Italian hand not unlike Mary's own. Gordon Daviot, the modern playwright, said that if she had seen Bothwell's handwriting before she wrote her *Queen of Scots*, she would have made him a very different character, 'for his writing was completely opposite of the man we have been led to believe in, being educated, clear-minded, constructive and controlled.' Throughout his tumultuous life, he was consistent: he did not change his coat, so that there was never any difficulty knowing which side he was on. He was not a bigoted Protestant but he was a true one: Mary could never prevail on him to accompany her to the palace chapel although she was successful with most of the nobles, and when he was married to the Queen of Scotland it was by the rites of his faith, not hers.

The Earl of Arran had never forgiven him for seizing Elizabeth's subsidy, and Bothwell baited him tirelessly. Arran loathed him so heartily, with his unwelcome challenges to single combat, that when Bothwell suddenly made conciliatory advances towards him, he was scornfully repulsed.

One day in March of 1562 Master Knox was told that the Earl of Bothwell wished to speak with him. Master Knox must have wondered what his visitor had come about. Bothwell was a Protestant who had been the faithful servant of a Papist Regent, and not the Protestant with kirk-fever who came often to visit a preacher.

Bothwell soon made him wise to the reason of his call. His host knew that for years now my Lord of Arran and he had been at enmity? As Knox, in his house in the Netherbow, heard everything that was going on, as all Scotland, far less Edinburgh, knew of the enmity between the two men, he could assure his visitor he did. It then transpired that what Bothwell had come to petition was: would he use his good offices to bring them together in amity and concord? He was finding it expensive having to be accompanied everywhere he went with a large following in case of attack from my Lord Arran and his Hamiltons, and was anxious to cut costs. Knox agreed, since it was wrong that two men of the one religion should live in such ungodly strife. Also his ancestors had been dependants of Bothwell's predecessors, and he felt bound to their young descendant by the ancient obligation of Scots kinness. But Knox was a shrewd man of the world, and while hoping for the best must have feared the worst.

The meeting arranged by the exhorter between the two earls took place in a Hamilton house in a district whose name has an ominous ring to it—Kirk o' Field. My Lord Arran was eccentric and excitable, so that no one was quite sure what his reaction would be, but when he saw his brother earl, he advanced hurriedly towards him and, stemming Bothwell's profuse apologies, warmly embraced him, exclaiming,

'If the heart be upright, few ceremonies may serve to content me.'

In days past when a Hepburn had met a Hamilton, there had been the clash of steel and people had fled to the safety of their homes. Now they paused in their work, came to their windows and doorways to marvel as two men passed on their way to the preaching—the Earl of Arran leaning lovingly on the Earl of Bothwell's protective arm.

A few days later Master Knox received another visitor at his manse, the Earl of Arran this time, in such a state of perturbation he could hardly speak. It was only with difficulty that the preacher could make anything out of his incoherence. At last he was able to gather that Bothwell had attempted to plot with his new-made friend, suggesting that he and Arran should kill Lord James, Secretary Lethington and anyone else who now misguided the Queen. She, he proposed, should be removed to stout Dumbarton Castle held by Arran's father, the Duke of Chatelherault, when he and Bothwell would rule all.

Since Arran had refused to have anything to do with the plot, Knox assured him he was salved of all blame. His advice was to keep silent about the whole affair, certainly not to write to tell the Queen as Arran was reiterating he was going to do. Knox knew Bothwell could attempt nothing alone, and he saw no point exposing an abortive plot which Bothwell would promptly deny. The Border Earl had one undoubted advantage over Arran: he was of sound mind, whereas it was obvious to Knox that his visitor, always unstable, was heading dangerously near the borderline.

Arran, however, was obsessed with the idea that he must get in first with the Queen before Bothwell tried to turn the tables on him. He wrote the letter. After all it was treason to conceal treason. She could but be grateful to him, would look upon him as her deliverer. Who knew but that his loyalty might cause her to seal the honour of their house by at last consenting to marry him?

After the letter had been safely despatched to the Queen, Arran set out for his father's home. The Duke of Chatelherault, an infirm man shivering with years, stuttered with fury when he learnt from his son what he had done, and railed at him that it had been dangerous folly to put such a thing on record. And Arran, in an agony now the letter had gone, craving to be soothed, to be told that he had done right, turned and accused his father of favouring Bothwell's treason.

When he went to his bedroom, his door was bolted on the outside: this was not the first time he had had one of his mad attacks. He tore the sheets from his bed, knotted them together and escaped through the window in his doublet and hose to a neighbour's house, where he told of his father's and Bothwell's treason and other undreamed-of things—devils, witches and suchlike.

No one feared the Earl of Arran now, but he was imprisoned to hold the powerful Hamiltons in check, while the custodian-ship of the Castle of Dumbarton was taken from his weeping father. He, crying like a child with grief that she suspected him, threw himself at Mary's feet. This was the man who with his falseness and treachery had been so sharp a thorn in her mother's side, of whom Mary as a girl had written, 'His words are finer than his deeds.' She, on her return to Scotland, had treated the Hamiltons with the utmost forbearance, knowing 'how many they were, and how allied.' The knowledge that she was free of them now can have brought her nothing but relief. But they were her kinsmen and she used them with all gentleness.

The Earl of Bothwell was also imprisoned, to the relief of Lord James who did not consider Scotland broad enough to hold them both. The captives were taken to Edinburgh Castle on the same day, Arran being carried in the Queen's coach because of his frenzy, and Bothwell riding beside him. So the Earl of Arran drives out of the story: he never regained his wits and in twilight solitude lived longer than any of the others who took part in it, dying twenty years after Mary.

The question that has to be answered is: which was speaking the truth, Arran when he told of Bothwell's plot, or Bothwell when he denied it? From what we know of Bothwell it is safe to say that he did attempt to make a confederate of his new-found friend. He must have heard the rumours flying about Edin-burgh earlier that Arran was plotting to kidnap the Queen, and they probably explain his uncharacteristic desire for Arran's friendship. With his dash and audacity backed by Arran's name, Bothwell might well think the plan could be successfully carried through.

Both men were imprisoned without trial, and for that Bothwell had to thank the Queen's Grace. Trials were summary affairs in these days, and Lord James was not likely to have him found innocent. Mary did not think him innocent either. She 'showed herself not a little offended with the Earl of Bothwell to whom she had been so good', but she providentially found an epigram in Livy when it came to asserting her prerogative, which stated that it was better policy not to try a criminal than to acquit him. She might be displeased with the rash Border lord, but she had few supporters on whose loyalty she could count and could have had no desire to see him eliminated.

If the Hamiltons were the most difficult Protestant family, the Gordons were the most difficult Catholic. The Earl of Huntly was the most powerful Catholic in the country, and held the important office of Chancellor. He was chieftain of the north, rich in lands and castles, and the Queen had been expected, as custom decreed, to make a progress north soon after her return from France, but she had never come. It was said she no longer smiled on the Cock of the North, who was adverse to the friendship with England which Mary, Lord James and Secretary Lethington were straining every nerve to strengthen.

Mary knew that a Catholic rising at that time would put an end to all her hopes of being named as successor to the English throne, but time spelt only one thing to the Earl—Huntly's time. He wanted to sweep before him, and his northern hordes, those Protestant toads, Lord James chief amongst them, set the Queen securely on her throne as a Catholic sovereign ruling over a Catholic people, with his son as consort beside her.

His eldest son was recently married to the Duke of Chatelherault's daughter, so it was on his second son, John Gordon, reputed to be the handsomest man in Scotland, that all his hopes were centred. But after a savage street brawl which ended in bloodshed, Sir John was clapped into the Tolbooth with almost as much satisfaction as Bothwell had been taken to Edinburgh Castle a few weeks earlier. Huntly's son, however, proved a restive captive, for within a few days he had contrived to 'loup-the-tether'.

People fell silent to ponder when they heard the Queen was to journey north that autumn into Huntly's land. Her brother was to accompany her—he was behind every step she took. It was said he would not rest until he had the Earldom of Moray—a Stewart never rested until he had what he wanted—but the old Cock would have something to say to that.

A great company, including Randolph, the English ambassador, was in her train as the Queen progressed into the Highlands. This was not France, where vineyards made the air wine-sharp. This was naked country which felt in decades not in years, in centuries not generations. Amongst the fields of thin whinnering corn, they came upon uneven cottages, clustered together as though for company, like pebbles at the foot of the hills. Spells were brewed in those smoke-filled interiors where they shared bed and settle with dog and fowl and supped nettle-broth, where they granted more allegiance to their chieftain than to their anointed Queen. Randolph found the journey 'cumbersome, painful and marvellous long; the weather extreme frost and cold; all victuals marvellous dear and the corn is never like to come to ripeness.' But Randolph was English, Mary a Scot, and there was something in her that responded to the wildness of this bare moorland scenery, battleground for the winds.

As the recalcitrant Sir John had omitted to enter himself in ward at her command, the Queen refused to be entertained by

his parents, the Earl and Countess of Huntly, who had sump-
tuously prepared for her, but passed within three miles of their
home. James Stewart and Lethington were both travelling with
Mary, and it was borne in on her that if Huntly were out of the
way it would do her no harm, for the Protestant English, whose
grace she was wooing, would view his downfall with no compassionate eyes. By appearing to aid his runaway son, Huntly was
giving her every cause for righteous anger and speedy retribution.

At Darnaway an order was issued against Sir John, who was
assembling men, and Mary created her half-brother Earl of
Moray. It is by this title James Stewart is best known to posterity.
Old songs sigh and ballads reverberate with the passionate hate
between the house of Huntly and that of Moray. A generation
later it was to be Huntly's hand, not Moray's, that gave the
death-thrust:

> Ye Hielands and ye Lawlands,
>   O where hae ye been?
> They hae slain the Earl o' Moray,
>   And laid him on the green.
>
> Now wae be to ye, Huntly,
>   And wherefore did ye sae?
> I bade ye bring him wi' you,
>   But forbade ye him to slay.

When Inverness Castle and Findlater were reached, they, in
the name of Huntly, refused entrance to their Queen. He and
his son were now looked upon as confederates and put to the
horn. Huntly, puzzled and afraid, fled, sending a lad with two
keys, one for the house of Findlater and the other of Auchen-
down, but his sovereign refused to accept them from such a
bearer. 'I have other means to open these doors,' she said, and
now in her train there could be heard the tread of soldiers' feet.

Danger put her on her mettle and she had a hereditary love

of a fray. Her hardiness amazed Randolph, accustomed to seeing her at court. 'I never saw her merrier,' he wrote, 'never dismayed, nor ever thought that so much to be in her that I find.' When she watched the soldiers come back in the morning from keeping the watch, she wished she were a man, to know what like it was to lie all night in the fields, or to walk upon the causeway with a jack and knapsack, a Glasgow buckler and a broadsword.

Huntly gathered his men on the Hill of Fare, but he did not rely on them or on his strategic position, which was good, for victory. He depended on the treachery of the soldiers mustered round the Queen.

The Queen's troops marched across Corrichie Moor in two distinct companies, one behind the other. Her brother was not sure of many of his men and those he doubted he placed in the vanguard; if they dared break ranks, the second force was charged to receive them.

Steadily, doggedly, the men in the first company were thrust on. Nearly every one of them had a piece of heath stuck in his helmet as a secret sign that he was Huntly's man. When the combatants met, they cast away their weapons and would have run, but Moray, with his relentless rear company, pressed them fiercely forward into the midst of the battle.

Huntly's soldiers were forced to leave the hill, and when he saw them struggling in the marshy, quaking ground at the foot, hemmed in and trapped on every side, he knew he was defeated. Men were crowding round him, thrusting others aside, putting out their hands to grasp his horse's bridle for the honour of taking him prisoner. He was corpulent and weighted with armour: with the intense excitement he fell dead.

His corpse was tried, and divested of his lands, heritages and goods; his dignity, name and memory pronounced extinct. Moray's title to the huge estates was now secure: he shared some of the spoils with Mary, and rich furnishings from Strathbogie were carried to Holyrood-house. Huntly's eldest surviving son, Lord George Gordon, who had taken no part in the strife but who had retired to his father-in-law's household, was ordered to the Castle of Dunbar, a prisoner for life. There was a current story that an attempt was made by Moray to trick the captain who warded him into executing his prisoner, but the captain insisted on confirmation from the Queen, which she refused to grant. Sir John and his young brother Adam were taken prisoner at Corrichie Moor. Adam's short seventeen years procured his pardon from his sovereign, but John, tied with ropes as though he were a common thief, was condemned.

Tongues were wagging, tongues that said the Queen had never consented to these proceedings, that they had been carried out against her will; tongues that whispered if Huntly had won the day she would have tholed her defeat blithely, and given herself to John Gordon. To silence once and for all such rumours and prove that she had countenanced what had been done in her name, Moray forced his sister to be present at John Gordon's mangled execution in Aberdeen.

> *But now the day most waefu' came,*
> *That day our Queen did greet her fill,*
> *For Huntly's gallant stalwart son*
> *Was headed on the heading hill.*

From that day something happened between Mary and her brother; both were probably unaware of it but their relationship was never quite the same. He still remained at her side, but never again was he to wield the same influence over her.

CHAPTER THREE

Happy be the bridegroom,
And happy be the bride!
And may not man, nor bird, nor beast,
This happy pair divide!

THE circle round Mary was narrowed, excluding those of her
own religion. James Douglas, Earl of Morton, son of her
father's bitterest enemy, filled the office of Chancellor in Huntly's place. Moray, Lethington, Morton—the three most influen-
tial men in her kingdom were now all Protestants.

Moray had far more in common with his English cousin Elizabeth than he had with his half-sister Mary, for he was more Tudor than Stewart, and the Tudors were realists, the Stewarts
romantics.

Her cousin's character was so opposed to her own that it was
some time before Mary could reconcile what she had hoped for
with what she found. The English Queen was capable of what
the Scots Queen was incapable, awaiting her time, she learnt by
experience and, lacking Mary's sweetness, was cynical. Where
she was parsimonious, Mary was a lavish giver who never
counted the cost. Both had courage, but Elizabeth's was tempered with caution, Mary's blazed like an unsheathed blade. Men
served Elizabeth, and fell in love with Mary. The unconscious
realisation of this explains, if explanation is necessary, Elizabeth's jealousy of the younger woman (Mary was nine years her
junior). Elizabeth felt as a woman and thought as a man. She
allowed others to make her mistakes, for she took so much into

account that she refused to come to a decision. To baulk the issue she changed her mind as often as the clock struck, a subterfuge which, whatever happened, enabled her to evade all responsibility. Mary was entangled in her own mistakes all her life.

Elizabeth was probably the only English sovereign up to her time who did not eye the crown of Scotland as a perquisite for herself: her strength lay in her concentration on being Queen of England. Protestantism meant little more to her than the means by which she had ascended and kept the throne, and a handy passport into other countries' affairs. She never evinced any interest in the permanent union of Scotland and England, or in the future of Protestantism in either. Her horizon was bounded by her lifespan, a sphere that sufficed Elizabeth who could not think of England as apart from herself or herself apart from England.

We now know nothing would have induced her to name Mary or anyone else as her successor. 'Think ye that I could love my own winding-sheet', she demanded of Lethington when he brought up the subject. But he and Moray, as Mary's chief advisers, knew the Scots Queen dare not relinquish her right to recognition as Elizabeth's heir-presumptive. Their country meant a great deal to both men, and it was important to them that it should receive its just place in the English succession. They knew Scotland could not stand alone, in solitary independence, in the Europe of their day: she had either to belong to the Catholic bloc or the Protestant bloc, and they were determined it would be the Protestant bloc. That meant alliance with England for Lethington: thus his dream of the two crowns united in one would come to pass. That meant alliance with England for Moray, to whom Protestantism meant much. And the succession would consolidate that alliance into perpetuity. Never again must Scotland be linked to France where the Duke of Guise, waging war on the Protestants in his own country, had once more ascended to power on the wings of victory, with Catherine de Medici and the boy-King in the hollow of his hand. Union with their neighbour England was the only alliance that would preserve Scotland's liberty and religion, and so fiercely did the Scots feel about religion that these two terms had now become synonymous.

But Elizabeth could not be expected to pronounce the Catholic Mary her heir-presumptive if Mary married a powerful Catholic prince, an eventuality neither Moray nor Lethington, nor indeed Scotland, wanted. Thus the succession theme became complicated by the marriage theme. If Mary desired to be named as Elizabeth's successor, Elizabeth must be allowed some say in whom Mary was to marry: she owed that to England, over the Border from, and joined to, Scotland.

Politically Mary was not only the daughter of her times, she was a Guise daughter and a Guise horizon knew no bounds. She did not allow the marriage theme and the succession theme to become overlaid: she played both to the top of her bent. While every effort was brought, directly and indirectly, to have her named as successor to the English throne, negotiations were once more opened through her Guise relations for her marriage to Don Carlos, heir to the Spanish King. They had been adjourned when Mary was in France, because Philip had not wished 'to marry his son to a process.' But now Mary was on the Scots throne, Philip was friendly to the project. Her claim to that of England was indisputable in Catholic eyes, and with England and Scotland annexed to Spain, both would be restored to the Catholic fold.

Mary opened her first Parliament in the spring. As she rode up the street to the Tolbooth, the people cried, 'God bless her sweet face.' A rumour had been spread that she had forgotten her native language or disdained to use it, so that when she spoke from the throne in her charming Scots the hall rang with the tumult of applause. Her tolerance of the new religion, her Stewart charm and grace of manner won the people.

It was long since they had witnessed such a Parliament and the sight was cheering to eyes little accustomed to pomp or beauty. The Queen had put aside her widow's mourning for the occasion and none outshone her, which was as it should be— 'The fairest rose in Scotland grows on the loftiest bough.' Amongst the ladies of the court and the wives of the nobility, the new Countess of Moray dazzled with jewels.

Only Knox looked on at the proceedings with a jaundiced eye. 'Such stinking pride of women as was seen at that parliament was never seen before in Scotland', he wrote. He claimed that the first matter attended to should be ratification by the crown of the 1560 enactments with regard to the change of religion, but Moray refused to press it forward. The preacher's tongue spared no one and he told Moray that the reason why he would not urge the Queen on anything she distasted was because he wanted Parliament to confirm his new earldom. It is not surprising that after this Moray and he did not speak to each other for some eighteen months.

Knox had that characteristic found in every great religious teacher, the belief that he is but the mouthpiece of God: Randolph commented that the preacher thought of himself as belonging to God's privy council. When it came to his ears, and everything came to Knox's ears, that the Queen might marry a Catholic, his pulpit was made a sounding-board for what the godly thought of such a project. His vehemence was such that he offended even Protestants: as the Queen's popularity rose, his was bound to fall.

Mary sent for him and he was reminded that she had asked him to exhort with her in private and not publicly before her subjects. When he replied that within his pulpit he was not master of himself but must obey Him who commanded him to speak plain, her tears dried into anger and she demanded his authority for dealing thus with her.

'What have you to do with my marriage', she asked, 'and what are you within this commonwealth?'

His reply comes trumpeting down the centuries to us, loud with the challenge of democracy, 'A subject born within the same, madame.'

In the anteroom of her cabinet he found some half-score of her ladies, Papists every one of them, and garbed in his eyes like so many peacocks. He looked at them from under his forbidding brow, and as he never could contain what he felt, he began to rate them soundly.

'Oh, fair ladies!' he exclaimed, 'how pleasing is this life of yours if it would ever abide, and then in the end that we might pass into heaven with all this gay gear! But fie upon that knave Death, that will come whether we will or not; and when he has laid on his arrest, the foul worms will be busy with this flesh, be it never so fair and so tender; and the silly soul, I fear, shall be so feeble that it can neither carry with it gold, garnishing, targatting, pearl nor precious stones.'

He was a little man in stature but he always seems to leave the air spent with the torrent of his words.

Mary had now the shrewdness and percipience of Secretary Lethington secretly aiding her marriage to Don Carlos—Secretary Lethington who liked to please everyone and sometimes ended in pleasing no one. He soared where others plodded, dared where others faltered, aspired after others despaired. That agile mind, leapfrogging difficulties, landed precariously on potentialities.

It was a dangerous game he was playing, for the powerful forces of Queen Elizabeth and Catherine de Medici were against the match, and he himself cannot have wanted it, whatever he pretended to the Scots Queen and those with whom he dealt.

If the Spanish marriage did materialise, what would become of his dream of perpetual amity between Scotland and England? What would become of Scotland's liberty and religion if she were allied to the most crushingly Catholic kingdom in Christendom? The only explanation for Lethington's part in the Spanish negotiations is that it was a feint: he was trying to force Elizabeth's hand, to frighten her into guaranteeing that if Mary did not marry Don Carlos the succession would be secure.

Mary's private secretary was a Frenchman and it was he who carried her confidential letters to and from her Guise relations. He was clad in deep mourning when he arrived from France that spring, bearing with him a letter from the Duchess of Guise telling Mary that her uncle, the great soldier-Duke, had been assassinated by a Huguenot.

The Guise family ties were strong; he was Mary's favourite uncle and she was stricken by the news. It was he who had said to her as a child, 'I recognise my own blood in you—you would know how to die well.' Another much loved, younger uncle died as the result of battle wounds a few days later.

These deaths cast a profound melancholy over Mary, and they were followed by that of her young half-brother John Stewart, he whose leaping and dancing had so scandalised the godly, who had said he would stick the preachers in their pulpits rather than see the Queen's Majesty troubled by their railings. She had wept for her want of assured friends when her uncles died, now she wept because those whom she loved best were always taken from her.

Mary could no longer depend on the support of her mighty uncle the Duke of Guise, and his loss to her was incalculable. The French Queen-Mother was now the power in the land when, after his assassination, she sided with the Huguenots.

But it was not her enemy of old, Catherine de Medici, who ruined for all time Mary's prospects of becoming Queen of

Spain, nor was it Queen Elizabeth, although both would have done so had it lain in their power, but one of her own kinsmen, a man of lofty height with a compressed dissatisfied mouth. It suited the Cardinal of Lorraine better to fall in with the Pope's and Catherine de Medici's plans than to advance those of his distant niece. Without consulting Mary, he agreed to substitute for Don Carlos as her husband the Archduke Charles, uncle to the Spanish prince, counting on his niece to fall in docilely with his plans. But to Mary the Archduke was 'poor, far off and the youngest of three brothers', no substitute for the heir to the Spanish throne. For the second time she saw her fondest dream of glory begin to dissolve before her.

Crops were late in the autumn of 1563 and ravaged by too early winter storms. Corn and wheat were trampled down by the heavy rains as though an enemy's army had ridden over them, and famine spread throughout the impoverished land. But what more could be expected with a Papist Queen daily enraging God with her idolatry and joyousities?

Holyrood, despite all efforts to make it brightly habitable, remained so comfortless and cheerless that Mary spent most of the bleak winter in bed to keep warm. She was ill that Christmas, and Randolph reported busily: 'Her disease—whereof it proceedeth I know not—daily increaseth. Her pain is in her right side. Men judge it to proceed of melancholy. She hath taken divers medicines of late, but findeth herself little the better.' Nowadays medical science would diagnose her symptoms as arising from a gastric or duodenal ulcer, which always recurred when she was upset.

Randolph little guessed the cause of Mary's melancholy was the news that the King of Spain, influenced by the Cardinal of Lorraine, considered the proposal to marry the Queen of Scots to his son at an end. These were dreary days for Mary. She was to try later to stir the dead ashes of the negotiations in an attempt to fan them into flames again, but not all her efforts could kindle even a glow of promise at which she could warm her ever sanguine expectations.

She now concentrated on the succession theme, and the Queen of England was asked to name the partner she considered most suitable for the Queen of Scots. We realise from our advantage-point of time that as far as Elizabeth was concerned there was not a man living suitable for Mary's husband. The English Queen had a marriage complex: physically or psychologically, or both, unwilling to marry herself, the jealousy the union of others excited in her was abnormal. Mary was a born match-maker, and delighted to grace weddings with her presence. Marriages at Elizabeth's court tended to take place in secret, and when she discovered what had happened, the bride more often than not found herself in the Tower.

Elizabeth's suggestion for a suitable husband for Mary was the offer of her own discredited lover, Lord Robert Dudley. Mary reacted swiftly to the insult by calling him Elizabeth's groom. The affair between him and the English Queen, which involved the death of his wife in suspicious circumstances, had been the scandal of Europe when Mary was a young bride in France. Elizabeth, to prove her sincerity and make him more honourable a match, created him Earl of Leicester in front of Melville, Mary's envoy, but somewhat spoiled the effect by tickling the new Earl's neck when she told him to rise. Mary asked Melville on his return what he thought of the English Queen's intentions towards herself and he replied with Scots directness, 'Neither plain dealing nor upright meaning, but great dissimulation, enmity and fear.'

Elizabeth, still unaware that the Spanish alliance would now never come to pass, wrote to ask her fair cousin to permit the Earl of Lennox to return to his native country. Twenty-one years ago he had been exiled from Scotland for treachery; now he had a straight young son, Darnley, who through his mother, Mary's aunt, was near to the English throne. Elizabeth's purpose for making this move was probably two-fold: to remind Mary there was another candidate for the succession should she prove troublesome, and to distract her cousin from the Spanish alliance by sending to Scotland a hopeful young man whom she could recall when she chose.

The Scots Queen gave her gracious consent for the Earl of Lennox's return, and after his arrival restoration to his estates was proclaimed at the Cross of Edinburgh. As other Scots nobles had been enjoying his lands during his protracted sojourn in England, his reappearance was not universally popular, but banquets in his honour followed each other in quick succession at Holyrood. He lavished costly gifts on the Queen, her attendants and the chief lords, and entertained right royally, doing everything a man with an end in view could do to ensure a fair welcome for his boy.

Her brother and the Secretary of State, in an effort to achieve something concrete for their sovereign, tried without consulting her to coerce Elizabeth into guaranteeing the succession if Mary married whom the English Queen might choose for her. But all their efforts led to nothing more tangible than Elizabeth's promise of what she might do *after* such a marriage, and neither man dared urge their queen to humble herself by taking a mean husband on such dubious safeguards. There was nothing to stop Elizabeth marrying herself, when the Scots Queen would be left with a negligible consort and, estranged from France, the loss of her rich dowries.

Moray and Lethington were in despair at the futility of their labours: 'the drift of time, delays from day to day, to do all for nothing, and get nothing for all.' They reported their lack of success to Mary and were surprised that their news had so little effect on her. But Mary was seeing through Elizabeth's tactics and expected nothing from her except what she would be forced to concede.

As she had dropped her brother from her confidence, so now she turned from Lethington, although both were about her as much as usual. She was handling her own affairs. Her French private secretary was dismissed for indiscretion, and one of her musicians, an Italian called David Riccio, put in his place.

She spent some happy carefree days at St. Andrews staying with her four Maries in a merchant's house, as though she were no queen but a burgess wife. It was February, when breakers left a frosted wave of foam on the wide shore and days gentle as spring are slipped in between the tides.

Mary was tuned to all her Maries' romances, and we can feel the atmosphere vibrant in the merchant's house where she lived so blithely with her little troop. She knew Mary Beaton's beauty had Randolph, the English ambassador, in its thrall, that her middle-aged Secretary of State was in love with Mary Fleming, that the sturdy Mary Livingstone had lost her heart to dancing John Sempill, whom Mary teasingly called 'your Englishman' because he was born on English soil.

Her Maries had laughingly vowed none of them would marry until their Queen did. And now making towards her was her cousin Darnley, on leave to Scotland for three months, at whom fate was pointing its finger since all suitable foreign matrimonial intrigues had failed. Through wintry weather on bad roads, he outrode all his followers that he could reach her on St. Valentine's Day.

It was one of Mary's characteristics that she did not accept a person as he was, with his limitations, powers and potentialities, but saw him clothed with the attributes she desired him to have. She liked her cousin more than she expected to like anyone sent by Elizabeth, and the more she saw of him the more she liked him. He was indeed a very presentable young man, tall and straight, with hair the rich yellow of buttercups, the Stewart long face and lily skin. His unbearded face made him appear younger than his nineteen years—he was three years younger than Mary—and this adolescence had a ripeness that might reach satiety before firming into the vigour of full maturity. Bred at the cultivated English court, he was well skilled in games and could play the lute with a grace that charmed his hearers. In many ways he must have reminded Mary of her first husband, and she would remember the happiness of her early marriage.

Darnley laid himself out to be pleasant to everyone he met in Scotland. Such an effort to appear amiable might make some think amiability did not come very naturally to him. He attended assiduously Master Knox's sermons, but the Protestants were not impressed, knowing that his mother in England was a strong Roman Catholic. He was grateful for anyone's good offices, in particular to Lord Robert Stewart who affably took him as his companion wherever he went, and Signor Riccio. He was a little man with lamp-like black eyes whom Darnley could always vanquish after a well-contested game of tennis, a droll little fellow quite unlike the courtly Secretary of State.

Lethington was in favour of the marriage. Moray's attitude took longer to form; at first he appeared to encourage it. No one could sit on the fence so patiently as he. Unfortunately when his half-brother Robert pointed out to Darnley the extent of Moray's lands on a map, Darnley exclaimed that it was too much—one of these tactless home-truths any family circle can do without.

Mary made one more bid to reopen negotiations for her marriage to Don Carlos: when it failed, Lethington was sent to England to gain Queen Elizabeth's consent to the Darnley union and to harp again on the old string of the succession, now made doubly sure since Darnley himself was so closely connected to the English throne. Never had Secretary Lethington been in such good trim as he was now: he wrote Cecil that he was in love and always in merry pin.

But even although the Scots Queen willed that they should be betrothed, the Earl of Lennox and his son had grave grounds for unrest. There were other powerful forces in Scotland opposed to the marriage, the preachers for instance, and the preachers would influence the people. Moray was less at court than formerly: he and Knox had healed the breach between them.

Darnley sustained his intense suppressed excitement as well as he could, but his ease of manner scarcely cloaked the secret tension he was feeling. It was discovered that he was sickening, and men grinned behind their hands when it became known that my Lord Darnley lay abed with measles.

Mary's nervousness lest anything should happen to him was soon allayed, for it was a mild attack. His recovery was as pleasant as she could make it, but it was fretted with anxiety when Secretary Lethington returned and news reached Scotland that neither Queen Elizabeth nor the English Council would sanction the marriage.

Mary acted at once. She procured the consent of her nobles, which was unanimous. Moray remarked afterwards that seeing the other lords had all voted in favour of it, he thought it best to do the same. But he climbed down from the fence a little later to appear on Elizabeth's side.

More than two months passed between the time Mary signified her intention of marrying Darnley and the actual marriage, and in that time the prospective bridegroom, who had no head for heights, revealed more than glimpses of his true colours. His elaborate court education served in his case merely as window-dressing: he was devoid of character to be developed, steeled, tempered. The honours Mary heaped on him did not make him honourable: unsatisfied as a spoiled child, the more she gave him, the more he wanted. Goodness can often be infused into badness; seldom can weakness be strengthened.

The marriage was hastened on because of Mary's fear that her glooming brother might try to prevent it. Her Cardinal uncle sent her word not to marry one who was a poltroon and a coxcomb, but Mary was long past the stage of taking advice from that or any quarter. He promised, when he knew her mind was made up, to procure the Pope's dispensation, necessary because she and Darnley were cousins. The marriage was not stayed when it did not come and Mary took Darnley for better or worse, with Catholic rites, without the dispensation, which did not arrive until months after the wedding.

Her betrothal to Darnley was the first irrevocable mistake Mary made, but the tragedy for her was it would not have been a mistake had Darnley been anything of a man.

The day before the ceremony, three heralds at the sound of trumpet proclaimed the bridegroom Henry Stewart, Earl of Ross and Duke of Albany, King of Scots. The proclamation fell on sullen ears and no one stirred in the waiting throng assembled round the Market Cross. Then one man, his hand uplifted, called out loudly, 'God save his Grace!' It was the Earl of Lennox.

CHAPTER FOUR

. . . As I stood looking on,
You drew your sword from out its sheath,
and slashed his body down.

AFTER the wedding there was a pause, like the interval that
falls when the cards, thrown on the table, are picked up
and redealt.

To allay Protestant suspicions, the King went in state to hear
Knox preach at St. Giles. He could have saved himself the trouble: Knox treated him on his throne as a sitting target and
preached a sermon of inordinate length from the text, 'Oh, Lord
our God, other lords than Thou have ruled over us.' The
preacher did not confine himself to Judah and the city of Jeru-
salem but illustrated his text with references to Scotland and the
city of Edinburgh, dwelling on the unhappy condition of a kingdom given over to the government of women and boys. There
were pointed references to the just punishment of Ahab who
allowed 'that harlot Jezebel' to do her will.

Darnley was in such a fume when at last he arrived back at
Holyrood that he had no appetite for dinner and spent the afternoon hunting. Late that evening Knox was brought from bed to
appear before the council, when Lethington told him he was
suspended from preaching during such time as their Majesties
should remain in Edinburgh. The suspension proved nominal:
a week later the King and Queen had left the capital with an
army.

Young Darnley, who had both Stewart and Douglas blood in

his veins, could claim kinship with the most powerful nobles in
Scotland. They gathered round him and the Queen to aid them
against her insurgent brother. Moray and the old Congregation lords, with the promised support of Elizabeth, were in arms.
The sides were taken.

Mary played the cards she found in her hands with an abandon and finesse that outmatched her opponents. She issued proclamation after proclamation, assuring her people of full liberty
of their religion, warning them not to believe her enemies if
they said otherwise, and rallying support to her cause. Her energy
and resolution were tireless: she rode with her men, and even
Knox had to admit that the Queen's courage increased man-
like so much that she was ever with the foremost. She sallied
through a storm of such wind and rain that trees were torn up,
rivers burst their banks and men were worn out. Darnley's armour was gilt, a foolish piece of foppery as he could so easily
have been singled out had it come to battle.

But this became known as the Chase-About-Raid. Mary pursued the rebel lords from place to place, doubling back to try to
catch them. They with their scanty forces, vainly waiting for
Elizabeth's promised help of soldiers and ammunition, kept on
the move. While Mary was looking for them in the west, they
entered Edinburgh, hoping for recruits, but although they
promised good pay to those who would fight for defending the
glory of God, there were few takers, and the cannon of the
Castle were turned against them. Knox, sitting quietly in his
study finishing copying out from memory the sermon he had
preached before the King, heard 'the terrible roaring of guns,
and the noise of armour did so pierce my heart that my soul
thirsteth to depart.' The rebel lords had to beat a hasty retreat
in the middle of the night.

The fact was they had over-played their hand. They had
counted on the support of the people and discovered too late the

Queen, not they, had it. They made for the English Border to await Elizabeth's help, whereupon the Earl of Morton took the Queen's army into Fife. He was not an incapable general but, a Lord of the Congregation, he was more a Moray man than Mary's, and it was probably because of him that the rebels were able to slip over the Border without even a running fight.

Moray made for the English court, but Elizabeth had no use for losers, particularly when she was chiefly responsible for their not having won the game. She had been led to believe Mary's rule in her realm was weak, instead of which the Scots Queen had carried all before her. Elizabeth found herself in the position she most dreaded, having shown her hand. The French and Spanish ambassadors alleged in their masters' names that the English Queen had been the cause of the rebellion, and that her only delight was to stir up dissension among her neighbours. A farcical scene took place when she forced Moray on his knees to swear in front of the ambassadors that she had neither aided nor promised them support. She wrote to Mary that she only wished she could have been there to hear how soundly she had rated him.

The other Scots rebel lords never forgave the English Queen for her treachery, but Moray did. Both he and Elizabeth were time-servers, and he understood her tactics. Within five months, on the eve of returning to Scotland, he wrote to his cousin that she had not in Europe a more affectionate servitor than himself.

For the time being all the tricks were with Mary, and already she had summoned two men to help her play her hand. Lord Gordon, who was wanted to raise the north on her behalf, was freed from the Castle of Dunbar, and Bothwell, who had escaped from Edinburgh Castle, was brought back from exile.

He had joined the Scots Guards in France, where he had nursed his bitterness against the Queen who had repaid all his loyal services to her mother by permitting him to be outlawed. He had sworn there were not the makings of one honest woman between her and her cousin Elizabeth. But he would have come farther than France, to aid the devil himself if need be, against her brother, the Earl of Moray.

On the voyage home, he narrowly escaped being captured by the English, but he arrived at last in Scotland to present himself to his sovereigns, heard again the voices of his countrymen, felt once more against his face the slap of the northern wind, blowsy as a fishwife.

The Earl of Moray was on the run when he arrived, but he was glad to find that another old enemy of his, Secretary Lethington, was not so great with the Queen as heretofore. A small Italian, his deformed body richly clad, one of two merry brothers, had more of her ear now. And at the Queen's side Bothwell saw a lad as pretty as any of her ladies-in-waiting.

As a child who had been allowed to stay up late cries when at last sent to bed, so he, given everything, expected still more. Not content with his title of King-Consort, he wanted it secured, in the event of the Queen's death, for himself and his heirs. He had forgotten about any goodwill he owed to Signor Riccio. Having to have a peg on which to hang his imaginary troubles, he blamed the quick-witted Italian for advising the Queen not to grant him the crown matrimonial.

Even if the Hamiltons had not been her rightful heirs, Mary would have hesitated to have complied with her husband's demands, for she had soon outgrown the mood when, in the first flush of their marriage, she had gloried in heaping on him everything she could, in humbling herself before him, and submitting her will to his. Too soon she learnt the quality of the man she had hoped would be her master.

He was very young for his nineteen years, this youth who was now King of Scotland. The power with which he had been so suddenly vested mounted to his head like strong wine. His position attracted to him men like his bastard uncle George Douglas, who acted on him as an evil genius. He lived at such a pitch that the present seemed to eat up the past and shut off the future. And once he had begun, he had to feed his life with excitement and riotousness; its thirsts could only be slaked by indulgence, its appetites by excess. He drank heavily to man himself, and insulted the Queen at a banquet when she tried to restrain him. The associates with whom he consorted revealed his likes and dislikes. He neglected his wife by spending his time with his own companions, so that she had to have a stamp made with his signature that deeds of state could be subscribed.

At court, after the wedding, nothing had been heard but 'the King and Queen', 'His Majesty and Hers'; now all that had changed to 'the Queen's husband'. His servants dreaded his fits of spiteful temper when anything went amiss with him. There were some things his parent, the Earl of Lennox, could neither buy nor bribe, and his house had never been trusted by the nobility. It did not take them long to discover that the son was worse than the father.

What with a Papist on the throne, an overbearing young loon they were told to call King at her side, and a wretched favoured foreigner whispering in her ear, the nobles were in a poor way. The pity was that the Earl of Moray could not be brought back to put things right again.

But the Queen refused to pardon him. Instead at the next Parliament he and his confederates were to be forfeited. At this same Parliament Roman Catholics were to be granted the same liberty of conscience as Protestants. It therefore became a matter of vital moment to everyone outside the Queen's party that Parliament should not meet.

The Protestants knew that mutual toleration between the two creeds was impossible: it must be one or the other. Once

Roman Catholics recovered a hold, there would be no toleration
for Protestants. Mary was no despot but she was a Roman
Catholic, and she must have hoped that the legal protection of
her religion would eventually result in its triumph.

Jumpy Protestants therefore read on the cards the attempted
restoration of the old religion and the extermination of the new.
There was the Queen's private secretary, David Riccio: what was
a humble Italian doing in the confidence of the Queen? They
had the distrust of all Scots for the foreigner meddling in their
affairs, for the man not born of the land. There is nothing to
indicate that Riccio had any connection with the Vatican, but
everyone believed he was in the Pope's pay. We do know that
Mary, her coffers depleted by the abortive warfare against her
brother, sent to the Pope for an adequate subsidy to restore
religion to splendour. There were rumours too that she had
signed the League of the Catholic Powers, and every Protestant
knew what that meant. The new Pope who sat on the throne of
St. Peter urged the Queen of Scots to restore her kingdom to
the Catholic fold. 'With the help of God and your Holiness,'
she replied, 'I will leap over the dyke.'

To criticism that she was insulated in her own secret coterie,
Mary could have replied there was no one outside it she could
trust. Morton was guilty of double-dealing, like all the treacherous Douglas connection. Lethington, with his English leanings,
was now suspect to his mistress. But she was sure of her small,
shrewd Italian secretary, she knew he put her first, that he was
a loyal servant. He was wealthy now, with the gifts of those who
desired him as a friend at court. It was said the Earl of Moray
had sent him a fine diamond, to procure his support with the
Queen for his return.

That her favour of him stirred jealousy and envy was inevi-
table, that it was unwise goes without saying, but there is not a
shred of evidence to confirm the calumny that she and Riccio

were lovers. Mary was neither dissolute nor promiscuous—her husband was both—nor had she any of Elizabeth's coarseness, but an innate sense of sovereign dignity and pride of race.

But the King, smarting from her refusal to grant him the crown matrimonial, was easily drawn into the plot that was now brewing, with the Queen's secretary as its focus. Riccio was deemed worthy of death because he was supposed to want to supplant Morton as Chancellor and the King was saying he was his wife's paramour. Darnley was the plotters' trump card: since the Queen would not cancel the Parliament that was to forfeit the rebels and grant liberty of conscience, the King must.

In December the Earl of Lennox wrote to cheer his wife, whom Elizabeth had sent to the Tower after her son's marriage, with the glad news that a royal child was expected. Within two months his son and he signed a bond with Moray and his confederates, now cooling their heels at Newcastle. In this document the rebels promised to take Darnley's part in all quarrels ('lawful and just quarrels' in some copies) 'with whomsoever it be', they were to maintain Protestantism and the crown matrimonial for Darnley. On his part, Darnley was to secure them from the consequences 'of whatsoever crime', maintain the *status quo* of religion and assist them to return to Scotland and their lands and emoluments.

Another bond was drawn up between the King and the Edinburgh ringleaders, the men who were to do the actual murder. They included Morton, Darnley's uncle George Douglas, Lord Ruthven and Lord Lindsay, all Douglas connections, for this was principally a Douglas plot. This document which Darnley's kinsman prudently extracted from him stated that the King assumed full responsibility for the murder of 'Rizzio the Italian, though he were in the very parlance and presence of the Queen.' If persuasion did not cause the Queen to yield to these matters, she was to be withstood.

Cecil knew of the plot, as did Elizabeth, but no whisper of it reached Mary, Bothwell or Huntly. The Scots Queen had restored all Bothwell's dignities to him and made Lord Gordon, who had raised a northern force, Earl of Huntly. Restoration to his northern estates was to be confirmed by the Parliament convened for March. Their common hatred of her half-brother, who had been the cause of Bothwell's imprisonment and the downfall of the Gordon family, drew the Border and the Highland chiefs together.

All Huntly's thoughts concentrated on how he could reconstitute the honours of his house. To achieve that he had to espouse the cause of the Queen who had allowed his father's and his family's ruin. The attitude of his youngest brother towards their sovereign was different. Adam was not seventeen when the Queen saved his life after the battle of Corrichie, and his personal feats for her in the future when she was in adversity were to flash with all the ardour and loyalty of shining youth.

Huntly had brought his mother and sister to court. His mother did all she could to further her son's ends, and was as discerning and propitiating in the circumstances as he could wish. His sister, Jean Gordon, was a pale girl about twenty: rather full eyes looked from her sloping face, and she held her full mouth firmly, in case it would tremble in spite of her. She was in love with Lord Ogilvie of Boyne but she was not allowed to marry him. Instead he was matched to that beauty of beauties, Mary Beaton, and the Queen made it known to Bothwell that it was her wish he should marry the Lady Jean Gordon.

In February of 1566, when last year's solitary leaves hung to the trees like shrivelled bats and the news the Queen was with child was on everyone's lips, the Catholic sister of the Earl of Huntly was wedded to the Earl of Bothwell with Protestant rites. He had insisted upon that, despite the Queen who wanted the marriage to take place in the Chapel Royal during mass. But

Bothwell would be bound to no woman by Pope's bands, and the wedding was solemnised in the Kirk of the Canongate.

The Queen, who was not sure of Huntly, hoped that the marriage of his sister to the Earl of Bothwell would consolidate the great forces of the north and south, but I do not think it was only insecurity of Huntly which prompted her to arrange the betrothal. It was insecurity of herself. No longer did she think of the Borderer as a nobleman who strengthened her footing in her realm. Unconsciously she was beginning to be attracted to him: he was a man and she was married to a boy. By assigning him a bride, Mary may well have felt she was propitiating the grudging fates for and protecting herself from hidden unformed thoughts. His marriage acted on her like a double-check. She herself supplied the wedding-gown, for she was one who had to adorn even the altars of sacrifice, and she had two new dresses made for herself for the betrothal festivities which lasted five days.

Bothwell engaged a French artist living in Scotland to paint his bride's portrait and his own—miniatures, as money was tight. Of all the women in his life, probably his pale young wife was the one who had the strongest hold on his regard. She was to divorce him that he could marry a queen. As we pick out the threads of that self-contained life, we find, instead of ends and pieces, that it is curiously of a piece, for many years later she was to marry her first love, Ogilvie of Boyne.

Bothwell took her to his Castle Crichton, which was an elegant home for a bride with its carved staircase, ornamented court and window-cases. But he returned to Edinburgh shortly after, to Holyrood where he found his brother-in-law, in preparation for the Parliament that was to be held early in March. In the procession Bothwell was to carry the sceptre, Huntly the crown.

Randolph wrote to Cecil that Davie, with the consent of the

King, was to have his throat cut within ten days, but the only
warning Riccio received was from an astrologer who told him
to beware of the Bastard. The Italian was not disturbed, thinking at once of Scotland's most famous Bastard, the Earl of
Moray, with the Border comfortably between them. He had forgotten about another bastard nearer home, George Douglas, the
King's uncle.

On the Saturday everything seemed as usual. The King
played a game of tennis with him in the afternoon. Then surely
was the time to murder him, if that were all that was intended:
the despatch of an Italian upstart would not weigh heavily on
the conscience of the sixteenth century.

There could be only one reason why he was taken in the
presence of the Queen, and that was in the hope she would
have a miscarriage. The murderers must have hoped for more
than that. The Douglases, and they were the planners, had an
ages-long hatred of the Stewarts. If the Queen died from shock,
the throne would be vacant for the wearer of the crown matrimonial.

Moray, with his whole company, was on the road from Newcastle to Scotland. The King had sent a large escort to convoy
them from the Border. To-night they would spend in Berwick,
to-morrow reach Edinburgh.

As twilight made furtive the streets of the capital, Morton
with a body of men surrounded Holyrood, filling the court and
guarding all entrances and exits. Inside, Bothwell and Huntly, in
their apartments, were having supper with Lethington, who had
been deputed to keep them employed and out of the way.

It was about seven and the Queen was having supper in the
turret room of her apartments. The cabinet is small but, perhaps
because we know of what happened within these panelled walls,
when we stand in it to-day, the empty cupboard-like room has
the resonance of an instrument. And there reaches us, with a

poignant immediacy, catches and asseverations of what was uttered here that wild March night strung at the end of centuries.

Although it was Lent, the Queen had meat on her plate, ordered by her physicians to keep up her strength. She was attended by her half-brother, Robert Stewart, her half-sister, Jean (the Countess of Argyle), Arthur Erskine, who was master of her horse, her French apothecary, one or two others, and some servants. One source says Riccio was standing at the sideboard eating something that had been sent to him from his mistress's table, another that he sat at the other end of her table. Candles lit the scene.

The King made an unexpected appearance. The seat on the Queen's right was vacated for him, but after he had kissed her, he preferred to stand leaning on the back of her chair. He had dined with three of the plotters, and his part was to lead them to the Queen's room by the private way from his apartments. The cork-screw stairs were steep and narrow, and one of the men, Lord Ruthven, was ill, so took long to climb.

He was the first to enter now, his face ghastly. A dabbler in black magic, he was dreaded for his sorcery. Everyone in that room must have known he boded no good, for he was in armour and wore his helmet, but Mary did not falter.

'My Lord Ruthven,' she deprecated, 'hearing you were still ill, I was about to visit you, and now you enter our presence in full armour. What mean you by this?'

'I have been ill indeed,' he agreed, 'but am well enough to come here for your good.'

Swiftly she retorted that armour was scarcely a proper habit for one who meant well. It was seen there were others behind him now in the narrow doorway.

'We mean no harm to the Queen's Grace,' Ruthven told her, 'nor to anyone, but to yonder poltroon Davie. It is he with whom I have come to talk.'

The Queen demanded what he had done.

'Ask the King, your husband.'

She turned to Darnley, standing behind her. 'You?' she questioned. 'You, my lord? Do you know anything of this enterprise?'

He shook his head and they heard him reply he did not. He spoke in French, 'Ce n'est rien! Ce n'est rien!' She faced the intruders again.

'My Lord Ruthven, I command you to go forth. You remain in our presence under pain of treason.'

Arthur Erskine and Lord Keith and her French apothecary moved against him but he waved a rapier and told them to lay no hands on him, for he would not be handled.

'I go forth only with that varlet,' he said. 'Let him come out of the privy-chamber where he has been over-long.'

There were other clamouring voices heard now, tramping feet in her bed-chamber without, the cries sickening to Stewart ears, 'A Douglas! A Douglas!'

'If my servant David has in any sort offended we shall exhibit him before the Lords of the Parliament to be punished——'

The voices began once more, movement stirred again in the outer room, and more men pressed into the crowded cabinet. The Italian, wild with terror, darted from side to side behind the trestle table.

'Take the Queen your wife and sovereign to you', Ruthven ordered the King, but he stood quite still, his big boy's face looking blankly about him, unable to pick up his cue.

The table between the intruders and the attacked man was thrown aside. The Countess of Argyle seized a candle-stick as it fell, mercifully holding it aloft, otherwise there would have been darkness. Riccio was behind the Queen now, pulling frantically at her skirts, screaming on her to save him.

'Fear not, fear not,' she cried to him, 'the King will not suffer you to be killed in my presence, nor will he forget your faithful services.'

She backed, her arms outstretched to defend him, towards the window embrasure until she was leaning back over the sill. George Douglas was said to have seized the King's dagger: he certainly struck the first blow over her shoulder, and her servant's blood spattered her clothes. They pulled his hands from her skirts by forcing back his fingers, until their victim shrieked with pain. They had ropes and dragged him, choking, from the cabinet, still crying for mercy and to the Queen to help him. Outside in the presence-chamber, and she must have heard them, they injured each other to get at his body. Fifty-six wounds were counted on his corpse.

Niceties that they had intended to finish him in the King's apartment and hacked him thus because they heard Bothwell and Huntly need not detain us. They left the King's dagger in the body to show who had sanctioned the act.

The sound of the uproar reached the brothers-in-law while they supped. They rushed out, Lethington following to keep up appearances, shouting on their servants to follow and calling on the cooks to bring their spits. The cry of 'To the Queen! To the Queen!' beat through the palace. But the men they found in the court were too numerous for their small band. It was explained to them about the removal of Davie, and they went back to their rooms. That night they escaped through a window which gave on 'the little garden where the lions were lodged'.

In the cabinet the King made his declaration against his wife:

'Suppose I be of mean degree, yet am I your husband, and you promised me obedience at the day of your marriage, and that I should be participant and equal with you in all things; but you have used me otherwise, by the persuasion of David— he whom you have been over-familiar with these past two months, who has dishonoured my bed.'

We know that Mary said to her husband, 'All the offence that is done me, my lord, you have the wite (blame) thereof, for the which I shall be your wife no longer, nor lie with you any more, and shall never like well till I cause you as sorrowful a heart as I have at present.'

The alarm of the town tocsin was heard and the marching of men in the courtyard outside. A voice of authority spoke from below the window:

'News of a disturbance is brought to the town. Is all well with the Queen's Grace?'

In vain Mary tried to reach the window; the strong arm of the dark-faced Laird of Lindsay held her back. The King was put forward to speak.

'The alarm is needless, my Lord Provost. Heed it not, and disperse. All is well.'

CHAPTER FIVE

Hush-a-bye, baby, thy cradle is green,
Thy father's a nobleman, mother's a queen.

THE following day, on Sunday morning, the King issued a proclamation dissolving Parliament. Thus the conspirators had won the stakes for which they had played. The Queen was their prisoner, the room in which she was locked was heavily guarded, no one, not even servants, allowed near her, her Roman Catholic secretary dead, and what they had done countenanced by and committed in the name of the King. They knew he was their strong suit, and that with him they could play the game as they chose.

Unfortunately for them, their opponent, the Queen, also realised where their strength lay. She knew she must separate her husband from his confederates, not only for the sake of her honour but that they might have no buckler behind which to shield themselves.

The King visited his prisoner wife at noon, the first of several visits, and was frightened at the state in which he found her. She told him she feared a miscarriage and that none of her women, French or Scots, had been permitted to attend her. He told her that he had never consented to Riccio's murder, only to his apprehension. Mary chose to believe him.

Darnley was weak and 'so facile that he could conceal no secret although it was to his own hurt.' Mary had little difficulty extracting from him the news that Moray and the rebel lords were on their road home and expected in Edinburgh that day.

She learnt from him she was to sign pardons for all the murderers, but was not to regain her freedom. While they ruled through him, she was to remain in their power and be sent to Stirling—Lindsay said she would have plenty of pastime there to nurse her baby and sing it to sleep.

Later Mary was to write that Darnley's heart was as wax. Now and in subsequent interviews she began to work on the impressionable wax that was her husband. Did he not see that all he had succeeded in achieving was the imperilling of their child's life and the murder of a good and faithful servant? Had he forgotten all her fair hopes and his fair hopes, hopes that their endangered child should rightfully inherit, of the English throne? Did he not see that they could have slaughtered anywhere, but did it in her presence knowing she was heavy-fitted? What did he think prompted them to do so vile an act? He could not imagine it was their devoted desire to further him. She asked him to reflect upon whom his ruin or preservation depended, upon seditious lords who were pushing him on to blast the tree, with no other design but to destroy the fruit, and crush him under the weight. What usage could he look for from men who had used her thus, their own anointed Queen whom God had set to rule over them?

And so she brought his fear into play, for Darnley was craven. What would he say to her people and her friends? Did he think her friends would submit to their Queen being imprisoned by murderers, doubly damned if her child died? Could he believe her subjects would brook their sovereign being held captive while murderers did as they listed? He knew Bothwell and Huntly had escaped. Did he imagine my Lord Bothwell would permit such heinous deeds to be done to promote men like Morton and Ruthven? Had he forgotten that Huntly, by raising his finger, could bring the north at his heels? What would happen to Darnley when she was freed and vengeance taken for this outrage? He would have to expect as short shrift from them, enraged by her wrongs, as he would have to expect from his Douglas kinsmen who would say they did all in the King's name.

Darnley was now as clay in her hands, even more pliable because he was made uneasy by the little regard his partners paid to him. Apart from dissolving Parliament and making his state toilet, he found he had less power than he had ever had. It was his confederates who commanded, he who had to defer.

Mary told him he must inform the murderers that any article she subscribed under restraint would not be lawful and therefore, if they wanted her to sign their pardons, they must remove their guards. But Darnley found he had the greatest difficulty prevailing on Morton and Ruthven even to permit her ladies near her, so afraid were they she would communicate through her women with her nobles or attempt to slip out muffled up like one of them. But at last they had to give way. She ate no food until four o'clock that afternoon, when Lindsay examined every dish that was taken in to her.

Their opinion of their royal prisoner's mettle was fully justified. Mary Livingstone carried to her husband, John Sempill, instructions to bring out of David Riccio's room the black box containing the Queen's foreign correspondence, and the important keys of her various ciphers. Old Lady Huntly passed to the Queen messages from Bothwell and her son, and a wild scheme to lower her from the window in a chair. But Mary knew this was impossible, because of the guards; besides she had formed her own plan, and gave Lady Huntly a note for her son and son-in-law. She was just in time, for the implacable Lindsay entered at that moment, ordering the Countess to leave and not return.

In case her fears were confirmed that her brother was in the plot against her favourite, Mary did not seek too closely, or attempt to cull any information from her husband, who was willing now to lay all he knew at her disposal. As well as separating

Darnley from the conspirators, another issue had presented itself. She must do everything in her power to prevent her brother joining, at least openly, the lords who had murdered Riccio, or they might prove too strong a band to break up. She sent him a message that when he arrived in Edinburgh she would see him.

He rode into the capital with his rebel associates late that afternoon, alighting at the Abbey. After supping at Morton's house nearby, he went to see the Queen. They wept when they saw each other and she greeted him as warmly as he greeted her, telling him as they kissed that well she knew if he had been at home he would not have seen her so incourteously handled. Both brother and sister knew that but for Darnley and his father, she would have had him back long ago; it was because of Darnley that she had quarrelled with him in the first place.

Nau, her French secretary, asserts that at this meeting Moray swore by his God he knew nothing of the murder of Riccio until his arrival. As Elizabeth and Cecil had both heard of the plot, as Moray had been in close touch with Morton during these past months, it is difficult to believe his protestation. Mary's brother was a master hand at not implicating himself; cautious and calculating, he was always careful to provide himself with an alibi so that he could arrive after the event and thus show a clean pair of hands. The best that can be said for either him or Lethington is that, knowing of the plot, neither would have been a party to the manner in which it was carried out.

He did everything that he could to aid his sister, meeting her every friendly overture with a gesture still more amicable. He mediated between her and the murderers, but as the hours drew on, the knowledge that he had at least known of the plot must have been borne in upon her. He, Morton and Ruthven knelt and perfunctorily asked for her pardon and less perfunctorily for restoration of their estates—always a Scots noble's most vulnerable spot. 'The loss of one mean man', remarked Morton, putting what he was thinking into a nutshell, 'is of less consequence than the ruin of many lords and gentlemen.'

Mary assured them she was never bloodthirsty, or greedy about their lands and goods, and promised to sign their securities if they drew them up. While they prepared their own pardons, she walked for the space of an hour in the outer-chamber between her husband and brother, then passed into her bedroom.

It was Moray who induced the conspirators to entrust their sovereign for that night to her husband's keeping. They, knowing she would sign no pardons so long as they remained, gave the articles to the King for the Queen's signature, and left the Palace. Moray returned with Morton to nearby Douglas House.

It was now Monday night, and Darnley had provided his own guards in place of those the conspirators had removed. Every care had to be taken not to raise any suspicions that could be reported to the supper party at neighbouring Douglas House, so the King and Queen went to bed in their separate rooms.

About midnight they rose. Mary, attended by a page and her maid, passed down the privy staircase to her husband's bedroom. With Darnley, they made their way to the pantry of her butlers and cup-bearers, Frenchmen all and loyal to a man. Elizabeth lived in daily suspicion of her servants but there was not one of Mary's, Scots or French, who would not have laid down his life for her. From the pantry a door opened into the burial-ground, at whose outer gate they were to meet their escort. The postern was fastened but in such a bad state of repair they were able to squeeze through.

The moon was up and the night fine. Mary faltered when, keeping to the shadow of the wall, they passed a new-made grave: it was where her Italian servant's mutilated body had been buried. At the gate of the cemetery horses were waiting, and three men: Sir William Standen, the King's English equerry, Arthur Erskine, her master of the horse and the hereditary shield-

bearer to the sovereign of Scotland, and Lord Traquair, her captain of the guard.

The Queen was lifted on behind Arthur Erskine; Lord Traquair took her maid with him; Sir William Standen and the
servant Bastien rode singly, like the King. The cavalcade of five
horses and seven people left the Palace and cleared the sleeping
town, passing the hump of Arthur's Seat. Darnley's nerve gave
and he flogged the Queen's horse pitilessly to make it go faster,
until she cried to him to remember their child. 'If this one dies',
he shouted, 'we can have others.'

At Seton House, ten miles distant, there were deep voices to
greet the Queen, and strong hands to lift her to the ground.
Bothwell, Huntly, Fleming, Seton and Livingstone, all men, were
in readiness for her. They waited only long enough to change
horses, and now the Queen rode by herself, with soldiers to ham-
per pursuit if need be and escort her to the fastness of Dunbar
Castle. Mary inherited her father's agility of body, the agility of
mind of all her mother's family, and a certain hardihood of her
own. As she rode the remaining twelve miles through the blessed
air, chill with dawn, she felt exhilarated and resilient. She was
safe, with friends, free.

As she wrote her letters, as proclamations were made in her
name and Bothwell raised the Borders, the lords in Edinburgh
woke up to the disagreeable realisation that their prisoner had
flown, their pardons were unsigned, their trump card, the King,
no longer up their sleeve but their opponent's.

Aimlessly they hung about, not knowing what to do and doing nothing. Lethington fled, then John Knox, minister of Edinburgh, 'departed from the said burgh at two hours after noon
with a great mourning of the godly of religion.' That seemed
the end. Glencairn, fellow rebel of Moray's, was the first to ride
off to sue for pardon. It was granted; wisely, Mary was willing to
forgive all but the actual murderers of Riccio. Lethington, whom

the Queen knew from Darnley had been in the plot against the man who had superseded him in her confidence, was stripped of the rich abbey lands of Haddington, which were returned to Bothwell who was again made Lord Admiral. Moray separated himself from the murderers at their own instigation, for now they were in need of a friend at court; and Mary won her brother's gratitude by signing his remission, but he was required to retire to his house. Huntly was made Lord Chancellor, as his father had been, in place of Morton.

The murderers fled to England, to Newcastle where, as Sir James Melville pawkily puts it, they found the other lords' nest warm, and at the head of three thousand loyal soldiers, Mary entered Edinburgh in triumph. A signed declaration was fastened to the Market Cross that the King never counselled, commanded, consented nor approved the murder of Riccio.

No one heeded Darnley either then or in the days to come. He not only publicly protested his innocence but denounced those he alone knew were in the plot. 'As they have brewed, so let them drink,' he said, but his anxiety to blacken his recent associates, most of whom were his kinsmen, did nothing to whiten him in his wife's eyes. When they heard of his signed declaration, they sent the Queen from Newcastle a copy of his bond with them, and from it she learnt the depths of his treachery.

He was too blameworthy, too near her, to appear even pitiable. Her coldness made him ill at ease and wonder if he had acted best for himself. His world became a sinister place, peopled by men, seen and unseen, who were his enemies. He could not think of a man whom he could call friend. He felt secure only if he were near his wife and she was irked to free herself of his company, but he followed her uneasily. Even under her grudging wing there were foes, for her friends had never been his. Because Darnley sensed his wife's confidence in Bothwell, he became as jealous of the Border Earl as he had been of her Italian secretary. Joseph Riccio was given many of his dead brother's appointments; he was more fiery than David, not so shrewd or willing a friend, and a deadlier enemy. There seemed no place to which a young King could flee to escape from frowning brows, chiding lips and chilling silences.

Mary could not bear the presence of her husband, but his absence only added to her anxiety. It was vital for her that he should patronise the birth of their child, for his absence could imply bastardy, yet rumours began to spread through Scotland that he was about to leave the country. The French ambassador wrote that all Queen Mary's people were barbarous, strange and changeable, that she had little confidence in them and there were few she could trust. She was depressed and weary, and as it drew near her time was haunted by the fear of Morton and his accomplices returning to disquieten her.

For her 'lying-in', she went to Edinburgh Castle, which was hurriedly prepared for her residence. Its rearing, rugged walls, that appeared to grow out of the very rock on which it stood, must have given her a comforting feeling of strength; but perhaps because of the impregnability of its position, the height of its plaster ceilings, the thickness of its solid walls, it seems separate from those who inhabited it. It lived on unchanged by the tapestries they hung on its bare walls, by the people who tramped up and down its Lang Stairs, who shouted and laughed as though to-day were all eternity, and gazed from its projecting oriels. One could bring forth a Prince of Scotland within its barriers and it would scarcely mark until decades later it would remotely recollect certain pangs, high hopes and long, weak cries. Aloof it stood, not furtive like Holyrood which, as if aware all the time of what was in store, had watched and waited. Mary must have wondered if she would ever enter Holyrood again.

The correspondence between the two Queens at this time was

at its kindliest, free of the dissembling insincerities of the past. Elizabeth admired a winner. She sent a message to Mary, wishing her short pain and a happy hour.

Moray was allowed back at court, and the Queen gave a banquet to which she invited Bothwell and Huntly. She drew from them all a promise to bury their discords in everlasting oblivion. It was the last public duty she performed before her child was born, the child who, if he were a son, would unite the rights of his mother and father to the English succession.

Any woman giving birth in these days was setting forth on a perilous journey from which she might never return, and Mary made her will as she waited to be delivered. No copies have been preserved, but she is said to have named Bothwell one of the commission of regency and to have omitted Darnley. She remembered her husband in the testamentary inventory of her jewels, which still exists, making him twenty-six bequests. Against the entry of a diamond ring enamelled in red she wrote, 'It is with this I married. To the King who gave it to me.'

The inventory is written in French: the words in the margin are blotched—'Remembrances for my well-beloved friends.' Mary was a bonny giver. She remembered not only bequests to the Crown of Scotland but to her servants, not only her kinsmen in France but her attendants, her connections by marriage, her illegitimate brothers and sisters, her privy councillors, lords and ladies. To Bothwell, her Lord Admiral, she left a table-cut diamond enamelled in black and a figure of a mermaid set in diamonds with a diamond mirror and a ruby comb in her hand. To his wife a head-dress, collar and cuffs, set with rubies, pearls and garnets. Her legacies to Moray and Huntly were costlier and more numerous. But if her child survived her, every bequest was to be revoked in its favour.

Her son was born between ten and eleven on the morning of the 19th June, 1566, the child who was to become James VI of Scotland and I of England, who was to sicken at the sight of naked steel. The guns of the castle announced the glad tidings to the citizens of Edinburgh, and that night five hundred bonfires blazed forth their joy.

Mary Beaton sped through the Castle to tell Sir James Melville, who was to carry the triumphant news to Queen Elizabeth. By noon he had taken horse, and was on his road to London. He covered the three-hundred and ninety-one miles between the two capitals within five days. The English Queen was dancing and merry after supper, when Secretary Cecil whispered in her ear news of the prince's birth. Instantly, as though touched by frost, her mirth shrivelled. She cried out, 'The Queen of Scots is mother of a fair son, while I am but barren stock.'

The day his child was born, the King, attended by Sir William Standen, visited his wife. Their voices reach us scarcely thinned by distance or time. There were many present to witness the ceremony of the Queen's presentation to her husband of the heir to the crown.

'My lord,' said Mary, 'God has given you and me a son whose paternity is of none but you.' She uncovered the baby's face. 'My lord, here I protest to God, and as I shall answer to Him at the great day of judgment, this is your son and no other man's son: and I am desirous that all here, both ladies and other, bear witness, for he is so much your son that I fear it may be the worse for him hereafter.'

The King flushed to the roots of his fair hair. To hide his confusion he bent quickly to kiss his child.

The Queen turned to Sir William Standen and said, 'This is the Prince whom I hope shall first unite the two kingdoms of England and Scotland.'

'Why, Madam,' answered the Englishman, surprised, 'shall he succeed before your Majesty and', it was the King's attendant who was speaking, 'his father?'

'Alas,' said Mary, 'his father has broken with me.'

'Sweet Madam,' put in her husband, 'is this your promise that you made to forgive and forget all?'

'I have forgiven all,' his wife told him, 'but can never forget.' Her mind strove with its memories of the night Riccio was murdered.

'Madam,' he pleaded, 'these things are all past.'

'Then', said Mary, 'let them go.'

BOOK THREE

Autumn

June 1566 – May 1568

Lord Darnley
By an Unknown Artist
Devonshire Collection, Hardwick Hall (National Trust)

James Hepburn, Earl of Bothwell
Miniature
Scottish National Portrait Gallery, Edinburgh

James Stewart, Earl of Moray
By an Unknown Artist, Holyrood Palace
By gracious permission of Her Majesty the Queen

Mary Livingstone
By an Unknown Artist
Collection of the Countess of Seafield

CHAPTER ONE

She began to shiver, and she began to shake,
She began to wonder, and she began to cry.

M ARY was twenty-three when her child was born, and had spent nearly five years in her native country. This hour which might have been reckoned her last, this moment when her long and painful labour was crowned by a son, was like a watershed in her life. As she lay in Edinburgh Castle where her mother had died, her heavy eyelids drooped, her narrow hands still, her voice faint answering the visiting ambassadors brought to her bedside, we can not only measure how far she had come but also understand why she chose to follow the road she did in the years before her.

For despite the seeming consummation of the moment, it was one of curious vacuum akin to reaction. She had saved her child's life in the face of wellnigh insurmountable odds and had given birth to a son, heir to the crown of Scotland, but that was all that could be marked up for her in the way of definite achievement.

Her succession to the English throne was as tentative as it had ever been. She was Queen of Scotland, but she ruled only by temporising with nobles most of whom she could neither like nor trust. Never had she been more beloved or esteemed by her people than now, but the *mystique* between sovereign and subjects was lacking. They loved her because she was the link between them and their old fierce race of kings, because she had given them a Prince of Scotland, but they could not identify

themselves with her. They identified themselves with the patri-
archal figure of John Knox; stalwart and unyielding as a tree, he
provided shelter. They were root of his root, branch of his
branch: the sap rose strong in him, and he fed them with the
living Word. This gracious flowering princess did not represent
them: it was said you could see the burgundy red in her throat
as she swallowed her French wines.

As for Mary, her illimitable horizons had shrunk into the misty
confines of her own country. She found herself tethered to what
she had thought of in the past as a spring-board. On her return
to Scotland, she had lived like a Guise, willing to sacrifice everything on the high altar of ambition, and for all her pains she had
suffered one overwhelming political disappointment after another, until tied to an inept husband, her Stewart nature took
over from her Guise intellect. From now on she was to act like
a woman, not a queen.

It was not unnatural that her long suppressed instincts when
given vent should veer towards Bothwell. He had served her
doughtily, and she owed him much, indeed, after Riccio's death,
practically all, yet he was not greedy for reward like others round
her. But that was not why Mary was to love him with all the
passion of her Stewart nature.

Her first husband had been, her second husband was, a boy,
Bothwell, a man. His masterfulness, his reckless courage, the
gaiety of his abandon, were all masculine characteristics that won
many women. Mary must have tried to make herself believe that
her dependence on this man was the dependence of a ruler on
a powerful subject, but a time must have come when she was
conscious of her pulses quickening in his presence, of ungrati-
fied moods when he was not with her. She, who started at his
footfall, could not have told how long she had known his step
from others.

We cannot say when she first knew she was in love with him,

but it was during the period between her child's birth and his christening, and there are hints and suggestions thrown up by the procession of events which enable us to spotlight the moment with some certainty.

The time was not conducive, with the Queen high on the wave of popularity, for Knox's return to Edinburgh. But Spottiswood, Superintendent of Lothian, was deputed by his fellow ministers to tell their sovereign of their gladness at the Prince's birth, and to ask that he be baptised according to the Reformed religion. Mary had no intention of granting their boon, but her relations with the Protestant Church were at this period happier than they had ever been. She herself gave the child to Spottiswood, who prayed for the heir of Scotland in his arms, playfully calling upon him to say Amen for himself. The child obliged by making a little cooing sound, and ever after the delighted mother called Spottiswood her Amen, as her son was to do when he could speak for himself.

Mary, who had her mother's tact, was careful to give the little Prince an entirely Scots nursery and household. A band of violers was appointed for him, and four ladies to rock his cradle. He was a fine boy, so stout and fat that the French ambassador, who was to act as proxy for his godfather, made play about how he would manage his weight at the christening, and Queen Elizabeth sent a merry message with her costly present of a gold font that if it were too small by the time it arrived Mary must keep it for her next.

His mother was determined that the christening of this child was to be an event of unparalleled splendour. She planned that each noble should dress his retinue in one colour, choosing green lined with red and gold for her brother Moray, blue lined with silver and white for Bothwell. She sat at her Exchequer 'to understand her finances', always a depressing procedure. But she was

able to secure at the Privy Council that she called a note of
£12,000 for the christening expenses.

After the birth, the parents appear to have been reconciled,
and Mary made Darnley the gift of a magnificent bed hung with
violet-brown velvet, cloth of gold and silver, enriched by mono-
grams and flowers sewn with gold and silver thread. It had curtains of damask, pillows of white satin, a blue taffeta quilt
stitched with crimson, and linen sheets from Holland. This was
the bed Darnley was to ask for in his lodging at Kirk o' Field
when he arrived to be purged of the smallpox; on this he lay
as powder was carried into the vaults below.

Reconciliation proved tenuous and the hunting expeditions
upon which the royal couple set out were enlarged to include
others, such as Moray and Bothwell, but sport was poor that year.
Darnley, not caring for his wife's guests, left early. He was
troubled she had restored her brother to her confidence, Moray
whose very shadow her husband said he distrusted. But we do
not need the contemporary English ambassador to tell us it was
not her brother who was the Queen's favourite, but Bothwell.
In her position, Moray was a necessity, and necessities are often
like the last resort—difficult to make friends with, whereas Bothwell could never leave her presence but she must have longed
to call him back. All the arrangements for the christening were
given into his hands.

Moray's shadow rested darkly on Darnley, who feared all his
former associates. And now the subtle Lethington was brought
back into favour, as though he had never had a long finger in
Riccio's murder, what Darnley was choosing to call 'yon foul
fact'. But the Queen needed the Secretary, who had the cleverest
brain in Scotland; only he could provide that liaison with England so necessary to promote her child's succession.

Darnley had the touchy pride of arrogant youth, the unre-
claimable obstinacy of one who will never admit he has been in

the wrong. It stung him to receive neither attention nor deference from the nobles, and it was always to his father's house he
retired to nurse his grievances and muse upon his wrongs. One
that grew more unbearable the oftener he turned it over was the
report that those representing Queen Elizabeth at the christening would be instructed not to pay him homage as King of Scots,
not to honour him at all. He was to be ignored as though he
were of no more importance than the English Queen's insignificant runaway subject. He did not think he could stand such an
affront before everyone, the foreign ambassadors, the Scots nobility, the whole world.

Copies of letters were conveyed to the Queen which Darnley
had written to the Pope, the King of Spain and the King of
France, complaining that the lamentable condition of the Roman Catholic Church in Scotland was due to the Queen's slack-
ness in furthering its cause. There seemed no lengths to which
her husband would not go to vex, injure and trouble her.

He was a boy fit only to flush and sulk, who strutted where
other men would have strode, smiled when they would have
frowned. His very presence raised in her a revulsion against him,
but once out of sight she was never sure what was happening
around him, what schemes others were putting into that oblong
head, what that foolish tongue was tattling. He held over her the
threat that he would absent himself from the christening, thus
branding their child a bastard, and as the event drew nearer, he
left his wife more and more alone.

That autumn the Queen attended the Justice Court at Jedburgh. It was her first visit to that part of her realm, and as she
journeyed towards the Borders, where Scotland and England
meet, the ground began to even out. The distant hills were gentle
enough to be called slopes, their contours rounded and smooth,
so that the landscape, uncomplicated by declivity or mountain,
had a certain simplicity about it. Although it was autumn, every-

thing still looked green, not the larch green of spring but the moss green of autumn.

She was travelling in the direction her grandfather had travelled when he had taken the ill road that cut through every Scots heart, that led over the Border to Flodden, the name that would always sound to Scots ears like earth filling in a grave. The flower of Scotland had marched beneath his banner, and there was scarcely a family in the land that did not record the name of one who had died with him.

Her court and ministers travelled with the Queen, but Bothwell was not of their company. As Lieutenant of the Marches, he had preceded his sovereign, to round up active Armstrongs and spirited Elliots who were to be brought to justice. Bothwell was a Borderer, he knew the bare ground and thin grasses of the marchland. A long line of Border men stretched behind his cradle, who had heard arrows sing in the south-west wind and learnt to fight without sparing, to glory in victory and to say to the enemy in victory or defeat before departing, 'God thank you!' Except for blood feuds, the Borderer avoided taking life; and although the English marchmen raided the Scots, and the Scots marauded and harried the English, there was little feeling of racial enmity between them. For they shared the common ground of the marches and could be trusted to keep its rules.

On her way, the dire report was brought to Mary that Bothwell had been killed by a well-known moss-trooper who had resisted arrest. If London and France, when they heard the news, reported that the Queen of Scots 'has lost a man she could trust, of whom she has but few', it can be imagined what the Queen of Scots herself felt. It was like her country losing its right arm. She hastened to Jedburgh, where she learnt he was not dead but gravely wounded. He was lying at his castle of Hermitage, some thirty miles distance, and after some days of holding assize, she went to visit her wounded lieutenant.

The ground her cavalcade rode over to reach him was between the folds of hills and over moorland. It was as though they were in a sea of it, miles of twisted heather roots, where wild cotton signposted marshy pools, black with peat. The Hermitage was an old windowless building standing on a hump of ground beside a Border river swollen with autumn floods.

Much business was transacted in the few short hours his guests, including Mary's brother, had with their invalid host. It was arranged that as soon as he could be moved, he should be brought in a horse-litter to Jedburgh, where his presence was urgently needed. Early in the afternoon the Queen and her company were in the saddle again, to make the return journey before light failed.

The day that had augured well, with a light frost that made sparkling bright the air, changed to wind and rain. Instead of their bridles ringing and jingling, their saddles creaked as the horses floundered and stumbled across the swampy moors. Their riders were soaked to the skin and caked and daubed with black peaty mud, as though thrown at them.

Mary was a practised horsewoman, and the ride of some sixty miles over difficult terrain might not have affected her had she not, since the birth of her child, been troubled more acutely by the recurrent pain at her side. Now when she arrived in Jedburgh, she was so ill that the soul-bell was sounded, and she lay blind, stiff and cold as a corpse.

Her symptoms, vomiting of blood, fainting and loss of sight, were compatible with advanced cases of duodenal ulcer. On the seventh day she made her confession and declared her adherence to the Roman Catholic faith. And now we see in the small Jedburgh house a scene such as that when her mother died in Edinburgh Castle. Mary called her nobles to her bedside, besought them to live in concord with one another, commended her son to their care and remembered her personal servants. She pled with her brother not to persecute the Catholics in Scotland after she was gone, and advocated friendship with France.

The following day her servants, believing she was dead, opened the window to let her spirit depart. Nau, her French doctor, states that Moray began to collect her silver and rings, which seems characteristic of her careful brother, although his recent biographer rejects the story as it does not strike him as very plausible.

I think when Mary rode between sunrise and sunset to Bothwell, wounded in his castle of Hermitage, she came face to face with the knowledge that she loved him. 'Would that I had died that time in Jedburgh', she was to say in after years.

Death was the one release from all the perplexities that fretted and the difficulties that threatened her, but Nau, 'a perfect man of his craft', would not let her be. They chafed, pulled and rubbed her numbed limbs, they wept and prayed over her rigid body, and when she sweated they, like peasants who have long supplicated God for rain, cried out with thankfulness.

She moved into the world again, forgot, as a healed body is only too anxious to forget, the pain and suffering it has endured. Her husband came to her but found there were no rooms for him to occupy in her quartering-house now the Earl of Bothwell was lodged there. Next morning he left, so cold was his welcome, feeding his resentful thoughts with mammoth plots and plans of what he would do one of these days to bring them all to heel.

Her illness left Mary mournful and dejected in private, but she was ever one who could spin the coin in public to show only her bright and shining side. The Border towns saw their Queen for the first time as she made her progress from one to the other. We know what she wore, little riding hats brave with a coloured feather, gay hoods, coifs, cauls and bonnets, gauntlet gloves

fringed and embroidered with gold and pearls, and regal front-
lets rich with gems.

The towns were clutched round their market cross, not yet
battered by time and weathered into a mere stump. In those
days buildings had not the importance they have now: then little more than shelters against the worst of the elements, like
byres or stables, they could be quickly rebuilt when the enemy
razed them to the ground.

The Scots Queen rode along her boundary as it marched with
that of England; no one could tell when the rivers in the De-
bateable Land ran red whether it were with English or Scots
blood. She saw the sentinel keeps and peels where Border men
scanned the horizon to watch for the first sight of the 'old
enemy,' bastions that more than once had been demolished by
English hands, no prisoners taken, no escape possible in that
derelict terrain, no quarter given and none asked. But always
they were raised again, to ward and watch, to warn the countryside by flare and bonfire to be at the ready—the English were
coming.

On a sudden impulse, Mary desired to see Berwick, and the
English governor, advised of her wish, met her at the Bound
Road. Pleasant was the talk between sovereign and governor as
they rode side by side to the summit of a hill, where the guns
of Elizabeth's Berwick-on-Tweed roared a royal salute to the
Scots Queen.

She did not return to Holyrood; since Riccio's murder her
Palace had become a place of ill-omen to her. Instead she journeyed to Craigmillar, two miles away. It was a castle standing so
high that it seemed to belong more to the upper air than to rocky
earth. With far prospects of the distant sea and arched by the
vast sweep of sky, there was health in its habitat that Mary
would never have found in low-lying Holyrood. She was still in
the hands of her physicians.

There was no privacy as we know it in castle life. The court travelled with the sovereign, and took up residence where she took up residence. Everyone knew when the Queen said, 'I could wish to be dead,' and when she received a certain letter from Darnley she cried out to her lords that rather than endure such sorrow she would slay herself.

She confided to Lethington that the root of her sickness was the King's ingratitude and misuses, that it was a heartbreak for her to think he should be her husband, and she saw no 'outgate' how to be free of him. The Secretary was a willing confidant. His urbanity made him sympathetic and he had always in the past tried to soften and mitigate circumstances for her if he could, crossing swords with Knox on her behalf. Now his gratitude for her forgiveness, the knowledge that the continuance of his power rested on her favour, combined to make her interests his.

It was at Craigmillar that the question of the Queen's divorce arose. To begin with, Moray and Lethington discussed it with one another. Both wanted Morton and his associates back: the Queen might be willing to sign the pardons for their part in Riccio's murder if she were promised a divorce from Darnley. They roused the Queen's brother-in-law, Argyle, in his bed to ask what he thought of it, sounded Huntly, and lastly brought in Bothwell. In a body the five men approached the Queen.

Lethington made a beginning by suggesting divorce: after all, the King was threatening to brand her baby a bastard, his immorality was a by-word at court, and a divorce could be procured because of his adultery. At once Mary pointed out her church would not recognise such grounds. Someone suggested annulment on the usual plea of consanguinity (Mary and Darnley were cousins). But Mary countered that her child might be proved illegitimate if her marriage were illegal from the start, and so lose the double thrones of Scotland and England. Bothwell sought to reassure her by citing the divorce of his father and mother, which had not interfered with his heritable rights, but Mary refused to agree to anything that could endanger those of her son.

She still had some feeling for the boy who was her husband because she asked what would become of the King after she had divorced him, which brought forth Lethington's ready solution that he could live abroad or in a remote part of the country. Mary's reply was one of utter weariness, but she must have known that her dilemma could not be solved by so temporary an expedient.

'It were better', she said, 'that I passed into France for a time and abode there until he acknowledged himself and is of a better mind.'

Lethington enquired if she could not depend on them, her principal nobility and council, to find means to quit her of her husband without prejudice to her son. 'And if my Lord Moray, here present, be little less scrupulous for a Protestant than your Grace is for a Papist, I am assured that he will look through his fingers and will behold our doings and say nothing to the same.'

Swiftly Mary replied, 'I will that you do nothing where any spot be laid to my honour or conscience. And therefore, I pray you, rather let the matter be, till God of His goodness remedy it, lest ye, believing to do me service, may possibly turn to my hurt and displeasure.'

Lethington closed the conference by desiring her to leave the matter in their hands, and assuring her she would see 'nothing but good, and approved by Parliament.'

One Bond, if not two, is believed to have been drawn up at Craigmillar, but what it purported no one knows. It was in Bothwell's keeping, and those who saw it spoke of seeing four or five signatures. All the men who had discussed her divorce with Mary signed it except Moray, but he was to look through his fingers. It may have provided not for Darnley's elimination but for his seizure to be tried for treason (warranted by his part against the Queen in Riccio's murder), but if that were the case, would not more nobles have signed it? The death of Darnley as a person was of little importance: the death of the King of Scotland raised it into quite a different category. Many of the men who had a hand in that deed were careful not to sign their names to it.

The variations that can be played on the theme of the Craigmillar Bond, or Bonds, are infinite: what we are left with as certainty is that it was there the first notes about the removal of Darnley were heard, and they were concerned with divorce. But human beings are so attuned that certain motifs, so startling when heard first, can be elaborated and built into a composition that at the end bears little resemblance to the score with which the players began.

Darnley visited Mary at Craigmillar and remained for a week, but the visit in no way bettered relations between them. Du Croc, the French ambassador, who was in the King's confidence as well as the Queen's, was convinced no good understanding was now possible between them, because the King would not sufficiently humble himself, and the Queen could not see any nobleman speak to him but she suspected some plot. The King told du Croc that he meant to miss the baptism.

Darnley was twenty-one that 7th October (1566); the following 8th December was Mary's twenty-fourth birthday, but no celebrations were held to mark either event. All roads led to Stirling Castle, traditional nursery of Scottish royalty, where the christening was to take place. The interior of the strong, dark hold reverberated like a drum with sound, and painted carved ceilings and tapestries made magnificent the royal apartments.

Darnley, who distrusted the governor of the castle because he was Moray's uncle, did not wish to stay there, but Mary overcame his reluctance. It was a triumph for her: even if he did not appear at the ceremony, he was with his wife and child.

Bothwell, who was to receive the foreign guests, was already in Stirling. Queen Elizabeth had sent the Earl of Bedford and a company of eighty gentlemen of England to honour the occasion; ambassadors from France, Savoy and Piedmont were present, each with his personal retinue who crowded the narrow Scots streets.

Darnley's father had filled the town with his supporters, and Mary, fearing a Lennox conspiracy, quarrelled with Darnley over it. Righteous and angry on her part, sullen and impenitent on his, were the words that passed between wife and husband while the whole castle was a-thrill with preparations for the royal baptism. Darnley flushed at something Mary said to him, which drew from her the remark, 'If you were a little daggered, and had bled as much as my Lord Bothwell has lately done, it would make you look the fairer.'

Brought up at the French court, she had arranged spectacles, mummings and masques, pageants and banquets for her guests. 'The service was great,' the laconic Earl of Bedford reported to his sovereign, 'and great welcome.' But the King, unable to face the English embassade, did not make an appearance. He remained in his apartments, hearing the feasting, the acclamation, the sound of music and the fanfare of trumpets, distant as echoes. 'The Queen behaved herself admirably well all the time of the baptism,' wrote the watchful du Croc, 'and showed so much earnestness to entertain all the goodly company in the best manner that this made her forget in a good measure her former ailments.'

On the christening day the barons of Scotland formed a lane from the door of the nursery to the door of the chapel royal. The wax candles they held in their hands made golden the baby Prince as he was carried by du Croc, proxy for the French King, young Charles IX, who was godfather. With him was the Countess of Argyle, who represented Queen Elizabeth as godmother.

At the open door of the chapel, Scotland saw what she had not seen for many a long day, what she was not to see again for centuries—the Roman Catholic Church. Waiting to receive the procession were mitred bishops in the full panoply of vestment and insignia.

The Protestant lords resolutely stopped: they would go no farther. Only three Protestant barons were actually present to witness the baptism of their future king. The others, Moray, Bothwell, Bedford amongst them, stood at the open door and watched.

Mary had her way. She heard the names Charles James pronounced over her child with the rich imposing rites of her own Church. All sighs and tears and dim reproaches lay beyond the chapel walls, like things that had happened long ago and now signified nothing. For all time this supreme exultant moment was hers. No matter what befell, nothing could take it from her.

CHAPTER TWO

I dree, I dree, I dropped it,
I sent a letter to my love
And on the way I dropped it.

JOURNEYS break up this chapter, sudden departures and
looked-for arrivals, halts at the houses of friends, a band of
exiles returning from over the Border, the Queen riding out of the
blurred distances into Glasgow, a few days later accompanying
a litter by easy stages because it was an invalid it carried. It was
the turn of the year and the cold unusually severe even for mid-
winter. The horses' footpads left smoke-blue hollows in the
snow.

The day before the first journey was taken, Archbishop Hamilton, who a week earlier had christened Scotland's Prince, had
privileges, removed seven years ago, restored to him. For exam-
ple, he could now judge of the validity of marriages within his
diocese and cases of heresy.

At once Knox, in England, was alerted to the dangers of Roman Antichrist recovering a foothold in his native country, as
was the Protestant court meeting in Scotland at that time. But
the Queen kept the Reformed Church quiet with a gift of £10,-
000 and 400 chalders of victual for the provision of their
ministers.

The renewing of the Archbishop's powers had a more personal
motive behind it than the attempted restoration of the Roman
Catholic faith: probably at no period in Mary's life did her religion mean less to her than it did now and in the months to

come. It was granted solely to give him power, by decree of nullity, to divorce—Mary from Darnley, say her apologists, Bothwell from Jean Gordon, say her detractors.

The great names of the Roman Catholic Church, such as Elphinstone and Wardlaw, rang only in the corridors of the past. The Archbishop, of the unstable Hamilton house, was an immoral man and a bad priest, the rotted fruit of a fallen tree. Beside him the ministers of the Reformed faith, the first of a long line of such men, emerge steadfast, courageous, uncorruptible.

On Christmas Eve, as a charitable deed suitable to the solemn festival, the Queen signed the pardons of Riccio's murderers. They were about seventy, many Darnley's kinsmen, and the most important was the Earl of Morton. Moray was anxious to have him home because his party needed strengthening to curb the power of Bothwell and Huntly; and Bothwell was anxious to enlist as many recruits as he could in the conspiracy gathering against the King.

It was probably at the time of the baptism that Darnley's murder was actually decided upon, not earlier at Craigmillar. How it was to be carried out does not appear to have been settled until comparatively late in the proceedings: gunpowder was eventually chosen, as the conspirators aimed at giving the impression the Queen's life was endangered as much as the King's.

On the same day the pardons were signed, Darnley left Stirling Castle without bidding his wife good-bye, and made for his father in Glasgow as swiftly as horse could carry him. Everyone was saying her benevolence was a Christian act in this season of goodwill, but the King did not relish such lofty forgiveness: he thought it was like opening the door to let his enemies in on him.

Wherever Darnley was rumours flew in the air, haphazard as fireworks. Scarcely had he left when it became known he was talking of seizing his son and undertaking the government of

Scotland in his name; he and his father were said to be assembling a force to carry out this purpose, which would include the
dethroning of the Queen.

In Glasgow the houses gathered round the cathedral as though
for protection. Snow covered their sloping roofs and piled on
the sills of their windows, darkening the already dark interiors.
A dread visitant was passing through many of the uneven dwellings—smallpox. High and low it visited, the rich and the poor
alike, for it stalked through Stablegreen Port and breathed on the
young King himself, laying him and his father low.

It was a particularly virulent type called by the common
tongue the purples. (There were those higher in the social scale
who believed it was not the prevalent smallpox which struck
down the King, but syphilis.) The Queen, when she heard of
his illness, sent her physician and asked if he would like her
to visit him; she had had smallpox herself, so was proof against
it. Everyone knew his answer before it reached her: 'I wish
Stirling to be Jedburgh, Glasgow to be the Hermitage, and I the
Earl of Bothwell as I lie here, and then I doubt not you would
be quickly with me undesired.' But he regretted his hasty words,
and she journeyed to Glasgow to visit him.

And now we come to the cross-roads in Mary's life, to which
every biographer comes: had she a share in Darnley's murder,
or was she innocent, with no knowledge of what was to happen
to him. I believe she knew, that her part was to take him from
his father's safe-keeping and bring him to Edinburgh, where
the actual murder would be men's work. There was no other
motive she could have to remove an invalid in the depths of
winter from his paternal home where he was receiving every
care.

Everyone knew that something was going to happen to the
King. Du Croc was not surprised when, on his return to France,
he was told of his death. Cecil was said to have known as much

about the Darnley murder as he had about that of Riccio. Some hours before it took place Moray left the court and went to St. Andrews—his wife, he said, was ill and he could not stay. Lethington was in the plot, and Bothwell one of the master hands in its execution; Huntly was spoken of as being at the scene on the night of the murder; Morton admitted years later that he had known of it; Archbishop Hamilton was a near neighbour at Kirk o' Field where the King lodged; it was his Douglas kinsmen who actually murdered him—and there was Sir James Balfour, the lawyer.

He is believed to have drawn up the Craigmillar Bond, it was he who persuaded the King to go to Kirk o' Field, who was said to have bought sixty pounds of gunpowder in Edinburgh before the murder, he who 'served with all parties, deserted all, yet profited by all.'

That Mary had no hand in the actual murder does not clear her, if she knew it was to take place and if it were through her agency that it did take place. I believe there is enough evidence in her behaviour both before and after the calamity to convict her. She does not stand or fall by the answer to the question whether she wrote the Casket Letters.

These are letters said to have been in Bothwell's possession, found in a small oblong silver casket, covered with green velvet, and bearing a king's crown and the monogram F (Francis, Mary's first husband). The casket held some letters and sonnets which her enemies swore Mary had written to Bothwell, and two documents relating to their marriage.

Now it is not only Mary's supporters who are chary about incriminating papers discovered at a crucial moment: from first to last everything about them reeks with suspicion. We have only copies, in French (the language in which Mary would write them), and in Scots and English translations. Only her enemies saw what they alleged to be the originals, and Mary was never permitted to have even copies of the evidence produced against her.

Of the letters, only that known as Letter Two need concern us, because if she wrote it from Glasgow to Bothwell when she went to visit Darnley, it is direct evidence that she was in love with Bothwell, that she hoped to marry him, that she had come to Glasgow with the sole reason of winning her husband's confidence in order to lead him to his doom. Even if it is believed to be partially genuine, partially 'doctored', it still indicts.

Perhaps one of the most important facts to consider when we come to decide whether or not Mary wrote, partially or wholly, the Casket Letters is that the same note of humility and dependence found in parts of them is found in others she was to write later to the Duke of Norfolk, whom she hoped to marry. The authenticity of Letter Two is accepted by most historians. It speaks for Mary as no forger could or would, for no forger would have put her case in so favourable a light.

The sonnets are rather unpleasant love-poems written in French, their theme that of 'the other woman' pouring out her heart to her married lover. Contemporary Frenchmen, poets like Ronsard and Brantome who knew the Scots Queen, repudiated her authorship: in their opinion the verses were too clumsy and unpolished to come from her workshop. Later French scholars aver that a Frenchwoman, which Mary was where language was concerned, would never have expressed herself thus. Gore-Brown believes the sonnets and letters were written to Bothwell by one of his mistresses, the daughter of a Norwegian admiral, and passed off with judicious doctoring as Mary's. But if her enemies were bent on forging documents, surely the last form they would choose to employ was a sheaf of sonnets. The faultiness of their construction can be explained by the tension under which Mary wrote them, if she did write them (and experts believe that the sonnets, as proof of Mary's passion for Bothwell, are less open to suspicion than parts of the letters). It must be remembered she was using a vehicle of expression to which she was unaccustomed, for the poetry she had been trained to write in her youth was artificial compared to what was being churned up in the crucible of her emotions.

That January day as she neared Glasgow, a village bounded on one side by a river and on the other a stream, she was met by retainers and gentlemen sent by her father-in-law, the Earl of Lennox, to wait upon her. They told her their master would not presume to come into her presence because of her recent unkind words regarding him. 'There is no weapon against fear', she answered sharply and, 'He would not be afraid unless he were blameworthy.' Mary held her father-in-law responsible for much of the distress his son caused her.

When she reached Glasgow, she did not lodge with her husband in his father's house, but in the archbishop's palace nearby with the Hamiltons who rode beside her. The world would split in two before a Hamilton ceased to hate a Lennox Stewart or a Lennox Stewart called a Hamilton by the name of friend.

Darnley greeted her warmly when she visited him, telling her he was so glad to see her he thought he would die from very gladness. His swollen face was badly blemished, he had lost his butter-yellow hair and he shrank from people's gaze. Because we know his days are numbered, he has become the victim for us now, as he lies on his sickbed thanking his servants for the least service they do him.

The Earl of Lennox was ill in another part of his house, and he sent a retainer to his son after his wife had left to find out what she had said to him. Through this man's deposition and Letter Two we know what took place between wife and husband when they were alone.

Mary asked Darnley what he had meant in one of his letters to speak of cruelty. It was of her cruelty he had spoken, Darnley told her, because she would not accept his offers and repentance. He admitted he had done amiss, but so had many of her subjects, and she had well pardoned them. He knew she could say she had forgiven him sundry times, and that he always returned to his fault, but he pled he was young. Could not a man of his age for want of counsel, of which he was very destitute, fail twice or thrice, and yet repent himself and be chastised by experience? If he might obtain her pardon only this once, he would not make fault again.

She was very thoughtful, which disturbed him. Unease can be heard in his remark that he has been told she has brought the litter with her. Yes, because she understood he was not able to ride on horseback: she had brought the litter that he might be carried more safely. He answered it was not meet for a man so sick he could not sit on a horse to travel, particularly in such cold weather. She replied she would take him to Craigmillar where she might be with him yet not far from her son.

He said he would go with her upon condition that they might be at bed and board together as husband and wife, and she should leave him no more. If she would promise that upon her word, he would go with her where she pleased. But if she would not, he would never rise from this bed.

Her answer was: 'It is for that effect I have come. If I had not been minded thereto, I would not have come so far to fetch you.' But before she could use him as her husband, he must be purged and cleansed of his sickness which she trusted should be shortly, for she was minded to give him the bath at Craigmillar.

'Then', he told her, 'I will do whatever you would have me do, so let me know your will.'

He did not want her to leave him, and besought her to watch by him, for he was sleeping ill, but she pleaded fatigue from her journey.

That night in the castle nearby, Mary began the letter to Bothwell which is known as Number Two in the Silver Casket series. She had only odd pieces of paper by her on which to write it.

'You have never heard him speak better nor more humbly; and if I had not proof of his heart to be as wax, and that mine were not as a diamond, no stroke but coming from your hand would make me but to have pity of him. But fear not, the place shall continue until death. Remember also, in recompence thereof, not to suffer yours to be won by that false race that would do no less to yourself.'

There is no evidence to show that Bothwell was as much in love with Mary as she was with him, indeed what evidence there is points to the fact that he was in love with his wife, pale Jean Gordon. Unconsciously Mary may have known this: her letter, like the sonnets, is that of one who is aware she has a formidable rival. What power would his wife not exert over him? What high resolve of his would she not intolerantly snap? What purpose would she not weaken with tears and reasoned pleadings?

'I think they have been at school together,' she wrote of her husband and her lover's wife. 'He has always the tears in his eyes. He saluteth every man, even to the meanest, and maketh much of them that they may take pity of him.

'We are tied to two false races. The good year untie us from them and God knit us together for ever for the most faithful couple that ever He did unite. This is my faith; I will die in it.'

Neither writer nor recipient realised they were being drawn by their own actions out of their depth, that soon they would be unable to control circumstances but instead be controlled by them. Inextricably involved one with the other, they were isolated by themselves. No longer was Bothwell one of many plotters, bent on the elimination of the King to help the Queen, or to pay off an old score of treachery. He had a motive unshared by any of the other conspirators: the Queen was in love with him. It was a role that did not fit him, for he was not a palace intriguer, but it was a role that ambition, pride and the gambler's recklessness forced him to play.

'Excuse me if I write ill, you must guess the one-half, but I cannot mend it, for I am ill at ease, and glad to write to you when other folk are asleep, since I cannot sleep as they do and as I would desire, that is, in your arms, my dear love, whom I beseech God to preserve from all ill, and send you good rest as I go to seek mine, till to-morrow in the morning that will end my bible. But it grieveth me that it should stop me from writing unto you news of myself, so much have I to write.

'Send me word what you have determined here upon, that we may know the other's mind, that nothing thereby may be spilt.

'I am weary and am asleep, and yet I cannot forbear scribbling so long as there is any paper.'

She spent the next morning working on a bracelet and did not return to her letter until evening when she could be alone.

'This day I have wrought till two of the clock upon this bracelet, to put the key in the clift of it, which is tied with two laces. I have had so little time that it is very ill, but I will make a fairer. In the meantime take heed that none of those that be here do see it, for all the world would know it, because for haste it was made in their presence.

'I go to my tedious task. You made me dissemble so much that I am afraid thereof with horror, and you make me almost play the part of a traitress. Remember that if it were not for obeying you I had rather be dead or I did it. My heart bleedeth for it. To be short, he will not come but with condition that I shall promise to be with him as heretofore at bed and board, and that I shall forsake him no more. Upon my word, he will do whatever I will, and will come, but he hath prayed me to tarry till after to-morrow.

'Alas, I never deceived anyone; but I remit me wholly to your will. Send me word what I shall do, and whatsoever happens to me, I will obey.

'He hath great suspicion, and yet, nevertheless trusteth upon my word, but not to tell me as yet anything. Howbeit, if you will that I shall draw it out of him, I will know all of him; but I shall never be willing to beguile one that putteth his trust in me. Nevertheless you may command me in all things, and do not esteem me the less therefore, for you are the cause thereof. For, for my own revenge, I would not do it.'

Between the lines we can read Mary's thoughts. The loathing with which she did this task would surely purify it. The turmoil and stress she was passing through would surely sanctify the knot with which later she would be tied to another; their faithfulness to each other ever after wipe out all the deception and pitilessness which had brought them together.

'I have not seen him this night for ending your bracelet, but I can find no clasps for it; it is ready thereunto, and yet I fear lest it should bring you ill-hap. Send me word whether you will have it, and more money, and when I shall return, and how far I may speak.

'Now if to please you, my dear love, I spare neither honour, conscience, nor hazard, nor greatness, take it in good part, and not according to the interpretation of your false brother-in-law, to whom I pray you, give no credit against the most faithful lover that ever you had or will have.

'See not her whose feigned tears you ought not more to regard than the true travails which I endure to deserve her place, for obtaining of which, against my own nature, I do betray

those that could let me. God forgive me, and give you, my
only friend, the good luck and prosperity that your humble
and faithful lover doth wish unto you, who hopeth shortly to
be another thing unto you, for the reward of my pains.

'It is very late; and although I should never be weary in
writing to you, yet will I end, after kissing of your hands. Excuse my evil writing, and read it over twice. Pray remember
your love, and write unto her and often. Love me always as
I shall love you.'

A few days later the King was carried from Glasgow. His face
was covered with taffeta, and he was borne on a litter at whose
side rode the Queen. Between Linlithgow and Edinburgh, they
were met on the road by Bothwell as Lieutenant of Lothian.

The expectation had been that Mary would bring him to
Craigmillar, which was suitable for an invalid, but Darnley had
no wish to go to a castle whose governor was one of Lethington's
brothers. He agreed to the suggestion of Sir James Balfour and
some members of his suite that Kirk o' Field would provide country air, for although close to the old wall of Edinburgh, it lay
amongst fields and gardens and orchards. James Balfour knew of
the very house; it belonged to his brother, and stood between
the ruins of two kirks.

Substantially built, it had a red-tiled roof, dormer windows
buried deep in thick stone walls, and crow-stepped gables. Floors
tilted, and draughts scraped below warped doors that swung on
unstable hinges. It was furnished hastily but richly for its royal
inmate, but it had stood empty for several years and must have
smelt of damp. Magnificent tapestries, spoils from Strathbogie,
the home of the old Earl of Huntly, were hung on the walls, and
he lay on the beautiful bed with its purple and gold velvet hangings which his wife had given him in the autumn.

There was a long hall, the prebendaries' reception-room be-

fore the church was wrecked by the English during their Rough
Wooing. It was used as a *salle* during the King's occupancy. His
bedroom was up a turnpike stair, and it had a small ante-cham-
ber. Immediately below was the room where the Queen slept for
two nights, probably to give Darnley confidence. Because the
house was built on a slope, the floors were at different levels and
the basement catacombed with cellars and storage vaults.

Bothwell's retainers later spoke about piling gunpowder, taken
from leather bags, in a heap on the Queen's bedroom floor, by
the light of a candle. But James Balfour's store of explosive must
have been placed in the vaults for the explosion was such that
'the very foundation stones were upheaved', and the whole fabric
reduced to a shapeless mass of ruins, 'dung into dross'. There
were many partners in the conspiracy which made synchronisa-
tion weak, but it is safe to say all fused into one against the
King's life. There were no counter plots as some have tried to
prove.

In the days that followed, Mary, who visited her husband each
day, nursed him so tenderly and entertained him so bravely that
any uneasiness he might have had was quietened. He had no
guard of his own as he had had in Stirling, but his servants passed
in and out of his room, and her friends and half-brothers came to
visit him. He had promised to love all she loved, and Bothwell
and Huntly and other lords used him both cordially and familiarly.

He despatched a letter to his father, still sick of the pox in Glasgow, telling him of his return to health, his good content and
the gentle treatment he had from his wife. In three days' time
his period of quarantine would be over.

Mary's half-brother, the ebullient Lord Robert Stewart, visited
him that day. They had been companions when Darnley first
came to Scotland, and the cords of that friendship still held, for

as the elder man took his leave he whispered to the invalid, 'Quit
this place or it will cost you your life.'

Darnley's blood must have run cold with horror. He told Mary,
there was no one else to tell, of what her brother had said, and
when Robert Stewart entered the room next day to ask the sick
man how he fared, he was confronted by the Queen. What was
this she was hearing, she demanded, about some plot?

Her brother did the only thing he could do in the circumstances, and that was deny that he had given any warning to the
King. At once a violent quarrel sprang up between Darnley and
his wife's kinsman, Darnley saying he had said it, Robert swear-
ing he had not, until Darnley leapt out of bed and both men
seized their swords. It was Moray who stepped in between his
half-brother and the King to separate them.

As though aware of what must have passed through his mind,
Mary was at her kindliest with her husband. Three days later
she brought all the nobles who had attended a banquet with
her to Kirk o' Field, to congratulate him on his recovery. We
see them move round his bed like court cards being dealt.

That night Mary spoke low and familiarly to him when they
were alone. Only once could his heart have missed a beat when,
talking of happy gentle things, he heard her say:

'About this present time a twelve-month ago—do you remember?—David was murdered.'

Bothwell is said to have entered to remind the Queen that
she had promised to grace her page's wedding-masque that night
at Holyrood. It was late, about eleven o'clock, when she left Darnley. To-morrow he would be purged of his illness, to-morrow
he could come and go as he willed. He told his servant Nelson:

'See you that my great horses are in readiness by five of the
clock in the morning, for I am minded to ride them then.' Was he
thinking of flight?

A little later he asked the servant, while he busied himself about the room, why he thought the death of that man should be called to remembrance to-night, when for long silence had been held on it? His servant tried to reassure him, saying it grieved him that such a thing had been said but his master should not let it disturb his rest when he had appointed to be up early in the morning.

The King, noticing he had a psalm book in his hand, suggested they should go merrily to bed singing a song, and called Durham and Taylor, his chamber-child or valet, to join them. They asked him to accompany them on his lute, but he said his hand was out for lack of practice.

The psalm they sang together was either five or fifty-five. Both deal with the wicked whose throat is an open sepulchre, who flatter with their tongue, whose words, softer than oil, are yet drawn swords.

They left him with Taylor, his chamber-child, who slept in the room with him. Nelson was one of his servants who was providentially saved.

Some two hours later the King was disturbed, it was thought by the sound of keys grating in locks as the murderers entered the house. His every instinct willed him to escape. He did not wait to put on his pelisse or slippers but carried them, as he leapt from the window on to a wall and from the wall to the ground. He hastened across the garden, his chamber-child stumbling beside him, but he was too late. His enemies closed round him and dragged him from the page.

He fought frantically to free himself as they tried to reach his mouth. He saw who they were, pressing down on him.

'Pity me, kinsmen, pity me for the love of Him who pitied all the world.'

He was tall and athletic, and he took long to die. To the very end he had the strength to struggle until finally they bore down on him and his beseeching voice was strangled.

CHAPTER THREE

Now they all sat or stood,
To eat and to drink,
And every one said what
He happened to think.

ABOUT two o'clock in the morning every citizen of Edinburgh town was startled into wakefulness by an untoward noise. Some thought it was the end of the world come at last and lay in their beds fearing and prayerful, but others, scarcely heeding to dress themselves, sped from their homes to find out what man was doing now.

The streets were crowded with people all hastening in the same direction from where the crack had come—to the house that lay between the ruins of two kirks. But there was no house there now. Yet only yesterday they had passed it as they walked down Thieves' Row and said to each other, 'See, there is where the King is lodging.'

The King! A-a-ah, so that was it, was it? It was the King they had blown up, God save his soul. Meg Fenwick saw the whole house rise in the air as if by black magic, the next minute it had scattered into fragments as though it had never been. And the King, the King, have they found the King? Sometimes these explosions do not do all the evil they set out to do. Ay, they found him, poor lad, in a garden nearby with his pelisse and slippers beside him, and his chamber-child—stark dead both of them, but, mark you, those who carried their bodies away said they were untouched by fire.

And whose finger's in this? Is there any need to ask? Barbara Mertane and May Crokat and John Petcarne saw a band of men hurrying away from Kirk o' Field—May Crokat caught one of them by the cloak as they shot past. Well, and what about that? The cloak was of silk. Ay, and they all wore slippers, fur-trimmed slippers, the kind of slippers you dance in with the Queen at a wedding-masque at Holyrood, the kind of slippers that are unco quiet in walking.

The voice of the common people was heard from the first, an anonymous sound that could not be coerced into silence, or weakened by the show of force. From close mouths and vennels it muttered and rumbled, gathering strength in the dark.

The Queen kept to her chamber that day and no one except those most familiar with her were allowed to enter. But the Earl of Bothwell moved abroad about the palace of Holyrood: there was of course nothing untoward about that; in those days the court moved with the sovereign.

'The Queen's Grace is sorrowful and quiet', he told Sir James Melville when he called. 'The strangest accident has fallen out whichever was heard of.' Was he trying, by sheer force of personality, to hypnotise the attentive ambassador into believing what he was about to say? 'Thunder came out of the sky and burnt the King's house, and himself was found dead lying a little distance from the house under a tree. I would like you to go up and see him, Sir James, how there is not a hurt or a mark on all his body.'

Sir James, with his insatiable news sense, did try to see the King, but by that time his body had been removed and he was unable to catch a sight of it. There is no doubt, however, that Darnley was murdered by suffocation when he tried to escape, and his body, by one of these curious freaks of fate, was untouched by the explosion.

A reward of £2,000 was offered for the discovery of the murderers; nevertheless, no one in an exalted position appeared anxious to know who they were. Nelson, the King's servant who escaped, was interrogated: the inquiry did not seek further when he stated that the servants of the Queen's Grace had the keys to the King's chamber. But voices could be heard in back courts and alleys denouncing the Earl of Bothwell as the murderer; placards proclaimed him and Balfour, Black John Spens and Joseph Riccio; and a bill, fastened in the night on the Tron Beam for all to see in the morning, declared that the smith who had fashioned the false keys to the King's apartments would, on security being given, point out his employers.

Other initials began to appear on the placards, initials written so big that there was no mistaking them. The painted picture of a mermaid was displayed with a crown on her siren's head and a sceptre like a fish's tail in her hand. When the Queen passed up the High Street, the market-women cried out to her, 'God bless and preserve your Grace, if ye be saikless (innocent) of the King's death!'

'What is a Prince without a People?' Mary was to question, but when she heard the voice of her people raised not against her religion but her, she closed her ears to it at her peril. As nothing had stopped her from marrying Darnley, so nothing would stop her marrying Bothwell although he had a wife she herself had chosen for him.

If she broke with her people, her nobility broke with her and not because of any part she had in her husband's death. The sixteenth century was not squeamish about such things, and assassination was an accepted method of despatching an enemy. In the eyes of the lords, the King had merely received his deserts, and Bothwell, despite public opinion which persistently named him as the chief perpetrator, was no more incriminated in the deed than many of them. But the nobility had not eliminated Darnley, or stood by and watched his elimination, to see Bothwell take his place: that was something they could not stomach. They broke with the Queen when Bothwell's kingship began to dawn on the Scots horizon.

Her party had never been strong; the men who nailed their flag to her mast were for the most part like Huntly or a Hamilton; they did so only because their destiny depended on her ship of state. To keep her afloat in the troubled contrary Scots political waters of her time, she had needed in the past her brother's steadying hand or Lethington's discerning weather-eye. Now she was to attempt to ride the storm under her own colours, jettisoning everything but the man she loved. Her very royalty made her regardless of consequences, as she ran up like a sail the divine right of kings in an atmosphere made increasingly dangerous with squalls from pulpit and people. The day-to-day events that chart her course as she went her own Stewart way hold for us a fatal fascination.

The remorse and horror she had felt before Darnley's murder no longer twitched and shook her when it was accomplished. She had wished him dead, and now that he had been removed she was incapable of pretending a sorrow she did not feel. Nor was there any point in keeping up pretence with those around her who had either been in the plot or had known of it.

The day Darnley was killed Mary's privy council wrote to Catherine de Medici to acquaint her of the fact, telling her the plot had aimed at the Queen's life as well as the King's. The letter was signed by fifteen privy councillors, including Lethington, who had probably drafted it.

On the same day Mary wrote to her ambassador in Paris, Archbishop Beaton. It is a letter hard and cold as flint, from which no sparks of sorrow, pity or regret are struck. 'This wicked enterprise', she calls it when she tells him 'we assure ourselves it was dressed as well for us as for the King; for we lay the most part of all last week in that same lodging.' Two nights she was known to have spent at Kirk o' Field. 'And was there accompanied with the most part of the Lords that are in this town that same night at midnight, and of very chance tarried not all night, by reason of some masque in the Abbey. But we believe it was not chance, but God, that put it in our head.'

The King was buried quietly one evening, when he was placed in the sepulchre beside Mary's father, James V. The Queen's defenders said the funeral was private because the rites were performed after the Roman Catholic Church; her enemies, that so secret a burial betrayed scant reverence for one who had been King of Scotland.

A room hung with mourning was prepared for her but Mary escaped from the depressing atmosphere of Holyrood, made melancholy for her by the murder of Riccio, now wellnigh unbearable after that of her husband. Her defenders said she did not observe the customary period of seclusion, the forty days of royal mourning, because Darnley was only king by courtesy.

She was accompanied to Seton, some miles out of Edinburgh, by her ladies and many of the nobility in her suite, including, like a grey shadow, Archbishop Hamilton. Bothwell and Huntly were left behind in Holyrood to guard the Prince.

It was noticed that the Border Earl coloured and kept his hand on his dagger when he spoke to anyone of whom he was not sure. The citizens saw him clatter up the Canongate with fifty horsemen galloping after to guard him. They watched him tear from the Market Cross a placard denouncing him as the King's principal murderer, heard him swear if he could find the author he would wash his hands in his heart's blood.

Even discounting the highly coloured, unreliable tales spread by Mary's enemies about her sojourn at Seton, the impression one receives of her during these days is not so much that of a newly made widow as hostess at an intimate house-party. It was a house-party that her brother refused to join.

If, when he was James Stewart, he found Scotland too small to share with James Hepburn, the Earl of Moray began to feel it uncomfortably cramped now Bothwell was beginning to be swollen into the biggest man it held. He made preparations to leave his native country, after drawing up his will in which he appointed the Queen and Bothwell his executors.

One receives the impression that already the rope was being fed to Mary and her lover, while Moray's will provided him with something like a safe-conduct should he return to Scotland when they were still paramount. Mary wept grievously at parting with her rather daunting brother, 'wishing he were not so precise in religion.'

That Mary had allowed her fibre to harden is shown not only in her disregard of public opinion but in her increasing insensitiveness towards her religion. She ordered rich vestments of cloth of gold to be made into curtains for her baby's cradle, and gave other church vestments to Bothwell to be cut into doublets for him.

Darnley's memory was now endowed with lofty virtues and a nobility that no one had noticed he possessed when he was alive. He was spoken of as 'gentle Henry' and 'that innocent lamb,' while Elizabeth began to refer to him in her letters to Mary as 'my slaughtered cousin.'

From Elizabeth in England, from Catherine de Medici in France, from her faithful ambassador in Paris, from her uncle the Cardinal of Lorraine, there reached the Scots Queen threatening, warning, sorrowful and anxious advice to seek out the murderers and exact rigorous vengeance for the crime. And nearer home there was the dead man's father, the Earl of Lennox.

Mary wrote to her father-in-law immediately after the death of his son, telling him of his fate. It was a conciliatory letter to which she earnestly craved a reply. She asked him to return to her court to help her to take proper measures for the detection and punishment of the crime, promising to treat him with the same affection that she had shown him on his arrival in Scotland. Her special messenger returned with Lennox's curt response that her Majesty's letter required no answer.

A few days later she heard from him. Weak and vacillating as always, he wavered between thanks for her comfortable letter and implied criticism that despite her labours to discover the offenders of this cruel deed, none had yet been named. He therefore took the liberty of suggesting that Parliament be called, when proper investigation could be made.

From Seton the next day, the 21st February, Mary replied she had anticipated his wishes—she had already summoned Parliament to meet on the 14th April. She signed herself 'Your gooddaughter Maria R.', good being the old-fashioned Scots, still heard in country districts, for in-law.

Back and forwards shuttled the letters between daughter and father-in-law. Waiting for Parliament to meet was going to cause delay, wrote Lennox; besides, this was not a parliamentary matter but of such weight that trial should take place immediately and be pursued with all diligence and expedition.

The trial of whom? asked Mary.

Of the persons named on the placards that were appearing all over Edinburgh, he replied.

The placards were numerous, she pointed out, and varied as to the names of those they denounced—on which did he wish her to proceed?

After sixteen days, during which pause Lennox wrote to Cecil asking for Queen Elizabeth's intervention (he may also have seen his one-time enemy Moray), he answered mentioning amongst others Bothwell, Sir James Balfour, and four of the Queen's domestics—'which persons, I assure your Majesty, I, for my part, greatly suspect.'

Like the calculated moves on a chess-board, strongholds began to change hands. To Bothwell was given Dunbar Castle, that stout place of retreat with power of escape by sea, useful to one who was not only commander of the Queen's military force but also her admiral. The great Edinburgh fortress, impregnable on its windy height, was also handed over to him, who was thus put in virtual possession of the capital.

Mary was not in a position to write to Lennox that those he accused would stand trial, and Bothwell attended the council meeting at which arrangements were made for his own assize.

The trial followed the set pattern for trials of Scots nobility, which were more parades of strength than anything else. Four thousand of Bothwell's supporters filled Edinburgh. Lennox with three thousand followers advanced on the capital, but on the way was told to proceed to the Council of Justice with only the number of attendants prescribed by law. As that was precisely six, Lennox was not unnaturally forced to turn. He wrote to the Queen pleading illness and for postponement.

Mary and her father-in-law had now changed places: it was vital for her that the trial should proceed and Bothwell be white-washed in public. Nothing was going to be allowed to stop its taking place, not even the Queen of England.

Something of the tension of that day of assize breaks through to us as we read of Elizabeth's messenger galloping up at six o'clock in the morning to Holyrood with a letter from his sovereign. In answer to Lennox's appeal, Elizabeth wrote urging her cousin to delay the trial (which in the past she had adjured her to hasten). But the bearer was not permitted to deliver his letter to the Scots Queen, whom he was told repeatedly was asleep.

He watched, cooling his heels outside the palace, the courtyard fill with men and horses as the bodyguard mustered to escort their master on his day of law. We can feel the atmosphere tauten, like a bow-string before the arrow is released, when Bothwell made his appearance.

A cheer broke from him as he headed the procession. He rode in state on a courser said to have belonged to Darnley, and the great company of friends who followed him were gay as those accompanying a bridegroom.

A servant of Lennox appeared for his master to request postponement on the grounds that he had not had sufficient time to prepare his evidence. He produced copies of the correspondence between Lennox and the Queen, which the Lord Justice, Mary's brother-in-law, despatched with the remark that from it the plaintiff requested summary action which he was now receiving.

The case was proceeded with. No 'verification or testification' being brought to support the charges, the jury withdrew to consider their verdict. It consisted mainly of Lennox's enemies, the Queen's friends and Bothwell's partisans.

After 'long reasoning' amongst themselves, they pronounced their unanimous decision, the acquittal of James, Earl of Bothwell. Much was made of a technical error found in the indictment which referred to the murder as taking place on the 9th instead of the 10th February.

In their congested town, packed with Hepburns and their spears, the citizens of Edinburgh watched the acquitted man ride by. They asked each other what they thought of the new-made widow's fiere, fiere being one of these Scots words which has half a dozen English meanings: a friend or comrade, a spouse, an equal or a match.

So they watched him go by, thinking they would have hung by the neck long ago. Maybe, but not all an earl's brave bluster would acquit him at the Assize of God, not all the horsemen in Scotland could win him from the gates of hell.

CHAPTER FOUR

I will be the fiddler's wife
And have music when I will;
Will, will, will, will.
T'other little tune, t'other little tune,
Pray thee, love, play me t'other little tune.

THE rumours flying around Scotland that the Queen planned to marry Bothwell reached as far as Paris, carried by English envoy and ambassador. It was also newsily reported that Lady Bothwell was refusing to resign her husband (they had been married for little more than a year), affirming that she would die Countess of Bothwell.

On the day Parliament met, the Earl of Lennox took ship from Scotland and sailed to England. It was noticed when the Queen attended, soldiers replaced the traditional escort of Edinburgh bailies in the state procession. Bothwell bore the Sceptre before her on the way to the Tolbooth, and the Sword on the return journey.

Parliament, in an effort to suppress once and for all these slanderous placards set up 'under silence of night,' imposed severe penalties if they were not destroyed by those who first discovered them. Their estates were ratified to the Queen's supporters, Secretary Lethington and many others were moored for the time being by large tracts of land: and the Protestant holders of various Catholic church lands, always so touchily ready to defend them, were confirmed in their possessions. But the most important statute was that by which the Protestant Church was practically established. Formal thanks were presented to the Queen for her tolerance, which left her without a party.

On the Saturday when Parliament rose, Mary returned to Seton, but Bothwell remained in Edinburgh, to preside that night at a banquet to which he invited the nobles and prelates who had attended Parliament.

And now the scene shifts from the Tolbooth to an Edinburgh tavern kept by one Ainslie. Instead of documents hung with seals, of sceptres, crowns and the royal signature, food and drink made lavish entertainment, and there were toasts and cheer. The host was at his most genial, seeing everyone's cup was primed. At that crucial moment when goodwill was at its height, before laughter turned to groans, when each guest felt warm and big with brotherhood, he passed round a piece of writing for them all to sign. Bothwell had the Scotsman's passion for legality, which papers history books with bonds and covenants, deeds and depositions.

The document came as no surprise to some of his guests, such as his brother-in-law Huntly, others can have been in no condition to read what they obligingly signed; the remaining signatories were either agreeable to adding their names or intimidated by the prevailing atmosphere of acquiescence. Of the company, one man alone did not sign, a Catholic earl who contrived to slip away.

We have only copies of what became known as Ainslie's Bond. In one made for Cecil, Moray's name heads the list of subscribers, where it would have stood had he signed before he left Scotland and which would explain his name taking precedence over those of Argyle and Huntly.

The Bond was carefully prepared and fell into two parts. The first pledged all those who signed to support Bothwell to the uttermost against his accusers (which Bothwell, knowing what he did about most of his fellow guests, would consider only his

due). The second clause pledged them to promote his marriage
with the Queen should her Majesty, now destitute of a husband, be so disposed. They undertook to look upon all those
who opposed such a marriage as their enemies and to spend life
and goods in its defence. This was the document to which eight
Roman Catholic bishops present appended their names.

Bothwell, flushed with success, the Bond with its shaky signatures in his pocket, joined the court at Seton. He therefore
witnessed the unpleasant scene that took place next day, when
the soldiers who formed the Queen's bodyguard mutinied in her
presence, demanding their pay. As one of the captains of the
Queen's guard, Bothwell should have known that the men's
wages were something like two months in arrears, but he lost
his temper and, in the unwisdom of over-confidence, caught
hold of one to strike him. Instantly the man's comrades rallied
to his support, so stoutly that the Earl was glad to let him go.
He tried to cover his discomfiture by rounding on one of the
officers, as the Queen ordered that the men be paid at once.

The Stewarts had never been rich although they owned vast
tracts of lands, and none had ever been able to afford a standing
army. Increasingly Mary found herself in the need of money,
which necessitated trying to elicit loans from France or a subsidy from the Pope. She was, too, beggared by her own gener-
osity, and she had supported Darnley since he had courted her:
his household, his band of English musicians, his extravagances.
Nor could her prospective bridegroom lighten her commitments
in any way, for he had suffered impoverishment because of
loyalty to her house which caused him to live beyond his possessions. Yet even knowledge of this somehow does not lessen
our sense of shock when we read that Elizabeth's christening
gift of the gold font was broken up to make coin.

The next day Mary left Seton to visit her baby at Stirling. A
small train accompanied her which did not include Bothwell,

who was mustering men—to punish some Border thieves, he said.

There had always existed between Mary and children a mutual love and confidence, that instantaneous understanding which calls forth the very thing it imparts. But her child was but a ten-month-old baby and had no memory of the mother he had not seen for some weeks. She was dressed in the voluminous mourning of her period, spreading cloak, wide hood, floating widow's veil, and as she, in her ardour, swooped to take him in her arms, he was frightened and drew away from her, crying.

She had not answered the letters of condolence she received but found time, although she remained only a night at Stirling, to write to the Papal envoy. With the knowledge weighing on her mind of what had been passed in Parliament the foregoing week and the irrevocable steps she was about to take, her letter is tense with anxiety. She entreated him to keep her in the good graces of his Holiness the Pope, and not to allow anyone to persuade him to the contrary of her devotion to the Catholic faith, in which she protested her intention to live and die, and declared her willingness to lay down her life for the good of the Church.

The next day she said good-bye to her baby. We do not know whether any premonition warned her that this was to be the last time she would see him. We do know that shortly after she left Stirling she felt so ill she had to take refuge in a roadside cottage. But she reached Linlithgow that night and slept in the palace where she had been born. The swans had returned to nest on the lake beside the palace, for it was April, when lengthening green twilights make the sky in that part of Scotland translucent as an egg-shell.

It was St. Mark's Eve, when fair maids throughout the country washed their smocks and prayed to good St. Mark to send them a husband. The Scots soldier, Kirkcaldy of Grange, was writing to England that the Queen had been heard to say she cared not to lose France, England and her own country for Bothwell (the sequence is worth noting) and would go with him to the world's end in a white petticoat.

Huntly was with Mary as she rode, and wisely kind Sir James Melville, and Secretary Lethington who looked suspicious, as though his long nose scented something in the air it was not quite sure it was going to savour. Of these three men only Melville was unaware of what was about to happen.

Did the Queen know, or was she like the rest of her train taken by surprise? Her modern supporters believe she was an unwilling partner in the events that now took place; her contemporary defenders excuse her compliance by asserting Bothwell was a worker of black magic and bewitched her (he was said to have studied sorcery when he was a student in France). But in our less credulous day we know that the only spell he cast over the Scots Queen was that of the man she loved. There can be little doubt she connived at her abduction and subsequent marriage, for she safeguarded her exclusive regal rights in a manner impossible to a helpless victim.

The abduction was necessary to the two participants who knew any lapse of time would be fatal to their mutual purpose—marriage. They had to make abortive the schemes already being made to frustrate their aim, and abduction alone guaranteed marriage so soon after Darnley's death. By the law of Scotland, the guilt of rape was effaced by the woman's subsequent acquiescence.

As her train approached Edinburgh, a great company of men was marked riding towards them with the Earl of Bothwell at their head. When he drew rein, he placed his strong hand on her horse's bridle, thus indicating she was his prisoner. He told her she was in danger and he was taking her to Dunbar where she would be safe.

The amazement suspended in the air was broken by one of
the Queen's followers who prepared to attack the Earl. Others
followed suit, drawing their swords and making a hostile movement forward. But the Queen would not have bloodshed, she
said, and thanked her followers as only she could, with praising
eye and gracious lips, sending the blood drumming in their ears.
She would rather go where my Lord Bothwell willed, she
averred, than that one drop of Scots blood be spilt.

She rode out beside the Earl, whose men dismissed her train,
all except Secretary Lethington moving somewhat restively on his
saddle, and the Earl of Huntly who appeared singularly at home
to find himself a captive, and devout Sir James Melville, who
was openly scandalised at what one of Bothwell's captains was
saying in his ear: that the Queen was made prisoner by her own
consent.

Mary, before she parted from her escort, sent a member of it
to Edinburgh to call the citizens to arms. This can only have
been for appearance's sake, but the man was desperately in earnest as he told the Provost that the Queen was being carried to
Dunbar. He insisted on the common bell being rung to summon
the burgesses to armour and weapons, and the trusty commander
of the Castle fired two of his guns at Bothwell's troops which
were, however, too far away to be hit. The hastily aroused
burgesses marched through the city gates but there was little
point going farther when they were on foot and those they pursued on horseback. They agreed amongst themselves there was
no help for the Queen.

In his lively memoirs Melville records that when they reached
Dunbar the Earl boasted he would marry the Queen despite
everyone—yea, whether she herself would or would not. It is a
pity for our sakes that the diplomat received permission next day
to depart, for his inside comments on what took place during

the ten days Bothwell held the Queen at Dunbar would have made interesting reading.

He was a shrewd, travelled Scot who was devoted to Mary and had a strong distaste for Bothwell. The raffish devil-may-care nature of the Borderer upset the puritanism of Melville, and it is chiefly his unrelieved portrait of the Earl which has blackened him for posterity. Melville did not believe in the authenticity of the Casket Letters and thought that, had the Queen been less summarily treated, 'process of time' would have cured her infatuation for Bothwell. It was his opinion that she had to marry him because he raped her at Dunbar.

Lethington remained at the castle, where he moved amongst his enemies with the politeness and agility of a cat. Bothwell had always hated him, the man of action's fear of the accomplished man of the world with his cool practised brain and rapier-like tongue. But Lethington knew the Queen would protect him: before they left Dunbar she stepped between him and Bothwell's dagger.

The Secretary waited at court, temporising as was his wont, watching how the wind would blow. He did not think like his fellow Scots in terms which were either religious or personal: he was activated by the politician's acute brain. He was attached to the Queen, but her chief importance to him was as a symbol of the union of the two crowns; and he remained with her as long as he saw her as that symbol. A past master at playing with fire, it was characteristic of his subtlety that while at Dunbar he was in secret correspondence with England, offering his services to Cecil and Queen Elizabeth, and with his fellow countrymen who had begun to band against Bothwell.

Even without Melville, we catch a glimpse of life at Dunbar. Bothwell discarded his mourning for the King and wore his finest clothes. He was seen out walking with the Queen, and it was

noted he was in lively good humour. They practised archery together, and rode side by side.

She had none of her ladies with her, but found at the castle
three women to be her companions. Bothwell's widowed sister
was one, she who married Mary's half-brother, the leaping Lord
John. Mary was fond of her and gave her presents of a sequined
crimson petticoat and a taffeta cloak; she also recommended her
fatherless boy for the vacant Abbey of Kelso, thus assuring him
of revenue. The other two were the Beaton sisters, aunts of her
lady-in-waiting, the lovely Mary Beaton.

Janet Beaton had been Bothwell's first mistress, although she
was much older, for she had a beauty of which even the years
could not dispossess her. The younger sister Margaret had recently acted as wet-nurse to the royal infant and was Mary's
confidante. Gossip and scandal tossed their names from lip to
ear, and both were credited with practising sorcery. Mary liked
her widowed sister-in-law better than she liked the Beaton sisters.

Proceedings for Bothwell's divorce were accelerated while
they were at Dunbar. Huntly prevailed on his sister to comply
and Bothwell entered into an agreement with his wife to endow
her with his favourite Castle Crichton and its lands which her
dowry had redeemed. She refused to accuse him of adultery with
Janet Beaton but named one of her own servants to procure a
divorce. The marriage had, however, to be dissolved by the Catholic courts as well as the Protestant, and Catholics did not recognise divorce.

In Roman Catholic eyes any union between the Queen and an
already married Protestant nobleman was as sinful as it was un-
lawful, but Mary chose not to listen to her confessor. It was
probably Archbishop Hamilton's fertile brain that devised a
method to procure annulment.

All the great noble families in Scotland were connected in
varying degrees by marriage; the relationship between Jean Gor-

don and James Hepburn was remote, but still required a dispensation to make their wedlock valid in Catholic eyes. Now the Gordons belonged to the old faith, and when the daughter of their house married the Border Earl they were punctilious to acquire the necessary dispensation. But at this later stage everyone chose to shut their eyes to that unwelcome fact, and Bothwell was freed from his wife on the grounds of an impediment that had been dispensed. Archbishop Hamilton used for the first and last time his restored privileges to declare null and void a marriage he knew was nothing of the kind.

Mary's supporters protest she was ignorant of the dispensation in Jean Bothwell's careful keeping, but she was a woman accustomed to rule and it is most unlikely she was unaware of any facet of the involved procedure. She married Darnley without waiting for a dispensation: she married Bothwell after his lawful marriage had been unlawfully dissolved.

Once the divorce was safely through, Mary and Bothwell returned to Edinburgh. They did not take the royal route from the Netherbow to the Castle, but entered by the more inconspicuous West Port. The soldiers who accompanied them did not carry their spears, as Bothwell was anxious not to give the impression the sovereign was his prisoner. He dismounted to lead her horse himself with every show of deference. Untrammelled by haste, almost sluggishly, the procession mounted the steep hill to the Castle, passed through the gates and was lost to sight.

The citizens of Edinburgh divided into two, those who said the Queen was the Earl's unwilling captive and those who said she was his most willing partner. Some said certain lords had offered to rescue her but she had chosen to remain with her seducer. Others wanted to know why, if she were free to come and go as she willed, she had been taken to the fortress and not to her palace of Holyrood.

All Edinburgh heard that Master Craig, colleague to John
Knox absent in England, was ordered to call the wedding banns
of their sovereign princess, whose husband was not three months
dead, and the man who was said to have murdered him. And all
Edinburgh knew he had refused to do so, until he saw the
Queen's signature that she was a free agent. Master Knox had
always said of course that no good would come of a Papist
Queen on the throne, and Master Knox's words had an uncanny
way of coming true. Scotland was still unsafe for him and they
missed the voice that put more heart into them than ten thousand trumpets, but Master Craig was keeping St. Giles warm for
his return from England.

The Queen and her seducer wanted to be married on Friday,
so it behoved them to waste no time and a signed assurance was
borne at once to the preacher. The Kirk Assembly then agreed
to proclaim the banns as was customary on the following three
preaching days, which ruled out the wedding taking place on
Friday. Who did this couple think they were, imagining they
could play fast and loose with the laws of the Kirk?

It became causeway talk that Master Craig had asked to speak
his mind before the bridal pair, but he was not granted the ear
of the bride. Bold and straight were his words to the bridegroom,
reminding him of the law of adultery, the ordinances of the Kirk
and the law of ravishing. He let him know that, with the sudden
divorce followed by the proclamation of banns, people were saying there had been collusion between him and his wife. And he
did not bridle his tongue when he reminded him of the suspicions about the King's death, which the marriage would but confirm. Soft and fair was the bridegroom's answer but the preacher
was not appeased. As for the people, they wondered why the
heavens did not open and discharge a thunderbolt, why the Lord
did not rain down lightning on such iniquity.

It was now that Bothwell made a decision that was to prove

disastrous to his and Mary's cause. As long as the fortresses of
Edinburgh and Dunbar, with their garrisons, stores and artillery,
were in his hands, he was strong and secure. But he relieved the
faithful commander of Edinburgh Castle and gave his post to
the corrupt James Balfour.

No one knows what induced him to take so fatal a step. He
may have resented the guns trained against his men when the
Queen was carried to Dunbar; or, more likely, Balfour may well
have blackmailed him into giving him the command. Bothwell
was vulnerable until he was actually married to the Queen, and
Balfour knew everything about the King's murder from the inside. He had had a hand in it himself, but was too wily a lawyer
to leave either finger or footprint.

A few days before her wedding Mary left behind her the
strong, thick husk of the Castle, which was so far above all her
subjects who lived below in house and hovel. As she passed
down the stony street on her way to Holyrood, they came out
of their awry dwellings and fiercely watched her go by.

She pardoned the Earl's abduction of her person and created
him Duke of Orkney and Shetland, titles his ancestor had borne;
few of the nobility were present to mark the splendour of the
occasion. The only articles he received from the royal wardrobe
were two cloaks of wild-cat fur to make him an evening mantle.

May was considered an unlucky month in which to marry, and
someone fastened a piece of paper on the Palace gates with six
Latin words which, translated, read: 'The people say That wan-
tons marry In the month of May.'

CHAPTER FIVE

It's like a pen-knife in your heart,
And when your heart begins to bleed,
You're dead, and dead, and dead indeed.

THE wedding, when a new-made Duke became consort of the
Queen, took place at Holyrood at the unusual hour of four
o'clock in the morning, not in the chapel but in the great hall.
They were married according to the Protestant faith, for the
bridegroom would submit to no other ceremony. He was so sure
of her, he made her unsure of herself. Amongst the witnesses
who signed the marriage contract were Huntly and Lethington.

The bride wore her widow's weeds, as she had done when she
married her cousin Darnley, but she did not lay them aside immediately after the ceremony as she had then. Those of the
populace who chose to attend the marriage feast saw the Queen
in her mourning sitting at the head of the table, and her new
husband at the foot. That was the only spectacle granted them,
for there was none of the joyous merry-making and celebration
to which they were accustomed when their sovereigns wed.

That she allowed herself to be married by Protestant rites troubled her greatly. She wept much on her return from the 'unlaw-
ful ceremony', and wrote to assure his Holiness that never again
would she, who had been nourished in the Roman Catholic
faith, leave it for her husband or any man on earth. But the
Pope was not so easily won: he refused to have any further communication with her until he saw better signs in both her life and
religion than he had witnessed in the past.

Du Croc declined to be present at the ceremony, although the Queen pled with, and Bothwell urged, him to countenance it with his presence. When he saw the bride and groom together later, he marked they were formal as strangers to each other and Mary told him that all she wished for was death. Alone with her bridegroom, she was heard to call for a knife with which to kill herself. Within a few days of her marriage her face had altered as not even illness could have altered it.

The prophecy of an old Highland witch spread through Scotland like wild-fire that the Queen's third husband would be dead within a year and she would be burnt to death within the lifetime of her fifth. The flames of speculation were not allowed to die, for the punishment for husband murder was the stake. That was the first time the smell of kindling faggots reached Mary, and she was afraid.

It is often more trying for the human spirit when the rope slackens than when life itself hangs upon it. And that was what happened to Mary Stewart and James Hepburn at the time of their marriage. No longer braced and steeled to pull against their common adversaries, they found themselves face to face with each other. As they looked, each would ask themselves, has it been worth it? So much for this—they must have wondered who was the enemy now.

The bride was jealous of the groom and the groom suspicious of his bride. He knew and she knew the yellow-haired, milk-skinned Darnley had been despatched not for his sake but for hers: it was Mary Stewart who had been unhappily married, not James Hepburn. She hated the thought of Jean Gordon living in his Castle Crichton as though she were still his wife, and he watched her closely—and those who came and went about her. He was distrustful lest his enemies—and he had scarcely a friend at court—her court—should try to form a nucleus round her against him.

He began to be an assiduous attender at sermons, and it is intriguing to wonder what kind of consort he would have made had circumstances been more conventional. It was revealed in the sermon preached at the wedding that he repented of his loose-living past and intended to turn over a new leaf. His statesmanlike letters to Catherine de Medici and Queen Elizabeth on his marriage are models of dignity and tact, and in the short space of time granted him he proved himself a constitutional, not a dictatorial, ruler.

Mary's world was changing round her: of her more intimate associates, Mary Beaton was no longer at court. Her aunts had quarrelled violently with Bothwell and the Queen; the enmity was dangerous because of the close friendship there had been between them. Bothwell's sister was now her principal lady-in-waiting, with her three other Maries still in attendance. Mary Fleming was even more blooming as the wife of Secretary Lethington than she had been as a maid, and she had never seen any reason why Mary Stewart should not marry the Earl of Bothwell since her heart was so set upon it. Huntly remained beside his sovereign but, shifting as seaweed to her uneasy gaze, he might drift out of sight altogether at any moment.

As the initial shuddering at the impact of their marriage wore off, Mary and Bothwell began to accustom themselves to their life together. In the month that followed their wedding we have a picture of an outward show of content and of their being quiet and merry with one another. They invited themselves to dinner at the houses of rich Edinburgh citizens, and when they walked out she hung on his arm. He paid her deep reverence in public, standing uncovered beside her, until she, with laughing protests, would take his cap and put it on his head with her own hands. He arranged a water pageant, called a triumph, to amuse the people, when she watched him ride at the ring and review the troops. There is an aching flatness, the effort of contrivance, about these May days merging into those of high summer, and no spontaneous surge of well-being.

It was a month of uneasy moves behind the good front presented to the world. Bothwell tried to transfer the governorship of Edinburgh Castle from Balfour to a reliable Hepburn kinsman, but the lawyer, secure in the knowledge that possession was nine points of the law, refused to be removed. The newly wed couple as they went in and out of indefensible Holyrood knew there was every likelihood of his treating with the enemy.

Mary, anxious to visit her child at Stirling, was told by his guardian, Moray's uncle, that she must not come with more than twelve in her train. Nor would his stepfather be permitted to see him, for he was suspected of having sinister designs on the infant Prince. These designs were probably no more sinister than that Bothwell wanted him to be brought up in France, but the precautions the guardian took cannot be considered unreasonable.

It was not her husband's death that brought about Mary's fall, it was her subsequent marriage. Stirling, with its focal point of Scotland's Prince, became the rallying-ground of these nobles who began to move once that marriage had become reality. Her brother Moray, as he travelled abroad, was warned to keep himself in readiness for their next letter.

Mary saw those confederate lords as traitors, banded together to lay the King's murder at her consort's door, when all Edinburgh knew there was scarcely a nobleman who had not that blood on his forestairs. They had signed a bond advising her to wed the Earl of Bothwell, but now they were determined to secure her liberty from him she had been through such travail to espouse. It was important from the lords' point of view to take up arms against the Queen's consort, not against the Queen, when they could be accused of lese-majesty. Their determination to guard closely the person of her son, Mary interpreted as their need of a seal for their rebellious actions.

As the circle inevitably narrowed round the royal couple, they turned to each other, aware their only safety lay in the other's strength. Mary's confessor, a Dominican friar, was the first to leave, asking to be allowed to return to his native France. Scarcely a day passed but there echoed through the galleries of Holyrood the departing footsteps of some nobleman who made his adieu with cold bows and averted eyes. The Master of Sempill and his wife, Mary Livingstone, one of her four Maries, took their leave of the Queen. The Earl of Huntly was heard to crave permission from his sovereign to go north, and brought upon himself bitter taunts that well she knew he meant to turn traitor like his father before him. Secretary Lethington made his departure with his wife so quietly by night that it was only in the morning it was discovered he had sped to join her enemies—Maitland of Lethington whose life she had saved with her own body, to whom she had given his very bride, rewarded past lapses with forgiveness, lands and high honours.

That day, when word reached them the lords were marching on Edinburgh, the royal couple left Holyrood, where Bothwell knew they could be caught as easily as bairns in a cradle. They depended on Huntly to raise the north in the Queen's name, and the Hamiltons the west; they themselves moved south where Bothwell hoped to muster men. He sent all his papers, plate and jewels to Dunbar and the Queen took with her a silver basin, a silver kettle and two thousand pins, so essential to a woman of her day.

They went to Borthwick Castle which stood on a high knoll, its sturdy tower looking squarely on the enclosing rounded hills. Their voices sounded hollow and unnatural under the lofty painted ceiling of its great hall, and in the swallowing space the figures of a tall woman and a vigorous man appeared stunted and foreshortened.

This was Bothwell's country; he belonged here, its people

were his. When he had been born, every footpath and landmark was already imprinted upon his mind. Only a mile's distance away was his Castle Crichton where Jean Gordon was still its lady. While he was at Borthwick with Mary Stewart, he visited his former wife at Crichton.

The lords sent a thousand cavalry to surround Borthwick which was impregnable, for there was no artillery in Scotland strong enough to reduce its walls of hewn stone. The insurgents shouted for Bothwell to come out, calling him traitor, murderer and butcher, and his servants had to hold their master back, so ready was he to accept their challenges. He had no intention, however, of being bottled in an unassailable castle with no forces to command in open field, and arranging with Mary to join him later made one of these hairbreadth escapes with which his life thrills. His sole companion was caught but he, not an arrowshot away, managed to slip through the enemy lines.

The Queen scornfully refused to join the insurgents in pursuing her husband, and answered taunt with taunt. They could think of nothing better to do than retire, leaving no followers behind to watch.

The next night, Mary dressed in men's clothes and, without gear or trapping, set out to meet Bothwell at their trysting-place in the wood. Together they rode through the darkness to the safety of Dunbar, the trackless moor and moss they traversed pricked with the innumerable infinitesimal lights of glow-worms.

If they had only remained there for a few days raising men the rebellion might well have petered out, for the capital did not rally to the lords as enthusiastically as had been expected. But the Queen and her consort received a message from Balfour, whom they did not know had already been gained by the enemy, which tricked them into setting out at once for Edinburgh, after spending only a night at Dunbar.

There were no robes in the fortress fit for a queen to wear;

indeed in the whole castle not a woman's garment could be found until one of the garrison brought her some of his wife's clothes: a short red petticoat, a coarse tunic whose sleeves were tied with bows, a muffler and a flat velvet hat.

In the humble dress of a soldier's wife, the Queen of Scots rode dauntlessly beside her husband, with a guard of two hundred and sixty men. Clothed in the *amour-propre* of royalty, her attitude towards the insurgent lords, in arms against their anointed sovereign, was as unyielding as it was righteous.

Scarcely any of her subjects obeyed her proclamation summoning them to her aid, but her heart and Bothwell's beat high as they moved through his country convening men, for reckless Hepburns and wild Hays flocked to their master. Her enemies noted that her increasing strength gave her high spirits. It was the middle of June, and the blue vault of Lothian sky dwarfed and made flat the earth spread so far beneath it. The last night husband and wife were to spend together was at Seton.

The following day they rode some thousands strong to Carberry Hill, about nine miles from Edinburgh, where the entrenchments of an old campaign still broke up the ground. For this was where the disastrous battle of Pinkie had been fought on that Black Saturday of Mary's childhood when the English, with their Rough Wooing, defeated the Scots.

Bothwell, who was a good general, took up an advantageous commanding position. He had a slight superiority in numbers, and watched the rival forces group on the rising ground opposite. Each side had to avoid having the sun in their eyes. A stream divided the two armies, so that whichever moved first was at a disadvantage; but even without this consideration, it suited neither to take the offensive.

Bothwell needed to play for time until the Hamiltons arrived with reinforcements, and the insurgent lords were even more reluctant to assault. They were not sure of Bothwell's strength for one thing; for another they were not anxious to take action against their sovereign. They maintained their quarrel was with her consort, and their tactics throughout the day were those of attrition and delay, to wear down and demoralise.

They allowed du Croc to approach the Queen on their behalf, bearing a ridiculous message the Frenchman did not deliver which challenged Bothwell to single combat with two, four, ten or twelve of their number, all of whom held he was the real murderer of the late King.

The ambassador found the Queen sitting on a boulder under the royal standard, which bore the lion and arms of Scotland. He paid her deep reverence and kissed her hand, assuring her that if she abandoned her consort the lords professed themselves her humble and affectionate servants who were ready to serve her.

'They show it ill', Mary replied with spirit. 'I would mind you that these same lords signed a bond recommending marriage with the man they now accuse of murder. They themselves vindicated him of the deed of which they now accuse him.' But Mary was a Stewart and the last thing she wanted to bring about was Scot to fight Scot. 'Nevertheless', she added, 'if they crave my pardon, I am ready to grant it.'

At this point Bothwell, who had been busy with his men, strode up. He and the Frenchman acknowledged each other, but no more.

'Am I the object of the rebels' hatred?' he demanded in ringing tones that his soldiers could hear.

'They profess themselves the Queen's servants', replied du Croc. Lowering his voice, he added warningly, 'and your mortal enemies.'

'What harm have I done them?' Bothwell wanted to know. He continued to talk loudly, like one who has nothing to hide. 'I never wished to displease any, but have sought to gratify them

all. Their words proceed from envy of my favour. But Fortune
is free to any who can win her. There is not a man of them but
wants himself in my place.' As he looked at Mary, something
about her disturbed him and abruptly he turned back to the ambassador. 'The distress of the Queen's Grace troubles me', he
said. 'To spare her, to save bloodshed, will you return to the
lords and ask if there be any man of good family who will step
out between the armies. I will fight him although I have the honour of being the husband of the Queen.' The Borderer placed
much store on these survivals, such as single combat and trial by
ordeal, of an older more chivalric age. 'I will meet him,' he said
with assurance, 'for my cause is so just that I am sure of having
God on my side.'

'I accept no such solution', the Queen interrupted quickly.
And she left no doubt whose side she was on when she said,
'I espouse my husband's quarrel.'

Du Croc, charged by the lords to arrange a relay of single
combats, agreed with the Queen that was not the solution.

'The time for parleying has passed,' said Bothwell, pointing to
movement in the enemy's lines which could indicate attack. He
suggested the ambassador should take up a position where he
could watch the greatest pastime of all, promising he would see
such good fighting that day as he had never enjoyed before.

Shortly the Frenchman replied that he did not look on civil
war as a pastime. 'I am bound to acknowledge', he wrote to his
royal master, the King of France, when he told him of the day's
happenings, 'that the Duke (Bothwell) seemed to me a great
captain, speaking with undaunted confidence and leading his
army gaily and skilfully. For some time I took pleasure in watching him and judged that he would have the best of the battle if
his men stayed faithful. I admired him when he saw his enemies
so resolute; he could not count on half his men and yet was not
dismayed. He had not on his side a single lord of note. I rated

his chances higher because he was in sole command. I doubted that the other side had too many counsellors; there was great disagreement among them. I took my leave of the Queen with regret and left her with tears in her eyes.'

The expected sortie came to nothing. It was midsummer and the day hot; the officers broiled in their armour. The royalist troops, tired with yesterday's long march, had no provisions with them and went to look for provender. Few found their way back: they were tampered with by the enemy who told them the Queen wanted to rid herself of her husband.

Bothwell, in an effort to force matters, marched his advance guard to the foot of the hill, and the rebels did likewise. No attempt was made to join battle. Mary, sitting on the boulder with Mary Seton, kept her gaze to the west, but the horizon was unbroken by the sight of oncoming Hamiltons.

Tullibardine picked up Bothwell's challenge and offered to fight him; the Queen, however, forbade the combat because he was a man of meaner birth and a traitor. Bothwell demanded Morton, his highest ranking adversary, and Morton accepted. On second thoughts, his friends telling him he was of more value than a hundred Bothwells, he chose a substitute to stand in for him. The Queen's husband was asked if he would give Lord Lindsay the combat. 'Lord Lindsay let it be,' he agreed.

Lindsay! His black face rose before Mary's eyes. Again she felt the iron of his hand before she could reach the window on the night of Davie's murder. Bothwell found he had to break down her resistance, but when he went to the appointed place to meet his opponent, Lord Lindsay did not make his appearance.

There was no longer any need for the insurgents to temporise. The day had worn on until the wheeling sun shone full in the royalists' eyes and, like mist on the hill, like snow on sodden ground, the Queen's and her lord's army was vanishing round them.

The rebels began a flanking movement. Bothwell tried to hearten what men he had to face it, but there was no fight in their depleted ranks. The battle was lost before it had begun, the enemy had won without striking a blow, and Bothwell knew it.

He tried to induce Mary to retreat to Dunbar, where he and what men they had could defend her; he warned her that her trust in human nature would be belied if she took the lords at their word. But she thought not of her own but his safety. She looked upon their parting as only a temporary expedient; she knew with Bothwell free anything could and would happen. To-day the hap was against them, to-morrow the die would be thrown in their favour.

The lords promised her allegiance if she separated herself from him, whom they would willingly allow to escape. The last person they wanted on their hands was one who could tell what part each had in the King's murder.

She asked for Lethington to discuss terms, but he was unable to face his sovereign, and the Laird of Grange rode up to represent his side. He was a fine soldier and he gave his soldier's word, on behalf of the lords, that they were one and all ready to honour and serve her, 'to yield to her all obedience next after God.' Mary stipulated that those who had taken up arms on her behalf should depart unmolested, and Grange's instructions were that her husband would be allowed to ride off the field unharmed and without pursuit.

Between two armies, Mary Stewart and James Hepburn bade each other good-bye. Her anguish and grief were great, and she wept and clung to him; many times they kissed. It was now he gave her the bond, said to be signed by Morton, Lethington and others, agreeing to the King's murder, charging her to take good care of that paper.

He put her from him and in a voice that onlookers could hear asked whether she would keep her promise to be his loyal wife. She could not speak, but nodded and gave him her hand on it. Then she watched him climb on his horse and disappear in a cloud of dust towards Dunbar.

CHAPTER SIX

What did I dream? I do not know:
The fragments fly like chaff . . .

NEVER had Mary Stewart been so alone as at that moment, and the terrible isolation of that midsummer evening at Carberry Hill clings to her throughout the remainder of her life until, twenty years later, she crossed the banqueting-hall at Fotheringay to the scaffold. Never again was life to swirl round her, and she at the heart of all its glad tumult. From now on she was as solitary as a spent moon, influenced by instead of influencing receding tides of movement.

She waited until Bothwell was well on the way before she allowed Kirkcaldy of Grange to lead her to the lords. We read that as she left, all her company scattered and went their way. But it was no unnerved, fainting sovereign who advanced towards the men grouped to await her.

'How is this, my Lord Morton,' she cried derisively as soon as they were within earshot, 'I am told that this is done to get justice against the King's murderers. I am told also that you are one of them.' When she saw Lindsay, she was as one beside herself. 'And you,' she said to him, 'ah, my Lord Lindsay, I will have your head for this.'

As she neared the ranks, she heard voices cry out at her approach, 'Whore!' 'Whore!' 'Burn the whore!' 'Burn the murderess of her husband!' She could not believe her ears. Two soldiers thrust the banner they carried between two spears before her, forcing her to look at it: her astounded gaze saw painted on it the figure of Darnley lying dead under a tree, while beside him knelt his baby son emitting the words, 'Judge and revenge my cause, O Lord.' Collapsing, she fell forward in her saddle.

Alone with thousands round her, she rode to Edinburgh, questioning if this were the way they paid her their promised allegiance and vowing she would have them all hanged and crucified, for threats were all that she had now with which to uphold herself. More than once Grange, who had promised her safe-conduct, had to silence with blows the more vociferous soldiers.

The burden of their cries was taken up by the townspeople of Edinburgh whenever she passed through the gates. They shouted and yelled at her from their windows, thronged the dark through-gangs, railing and menacing as she went by, shaking their fists at her from their stairheads. She was within spitting distance of them, for the tortuous wynds through which she was thrust were so narrow the soldiers following had to file past one by one.

Still dressed in the shabby clothes of the trooper's wife, the red tunic hardly reaching below her knees, her face was blackened with dust and tears. Once or twice she caught sight of a gentleman standing, richly clothed, amongst the humbly clad mob and cried out imploringly to him as she passed, 'I am your Queen, your own native princess; oh, suffer me not to be abused thus!' But always she was forced onwards by the press of soldiers following her.

She was not taken to her palace of Holyrood as she had expected but to the provost's house. As she climbed the high steps, a woman's voice was heard to call out, 'God bless her!' She was put into a small stone chamber, facing the street, which her guards shared with her.

When daybreak lightened the room, the noise outside, quietened although never stilled through the dragged-out night, rose clamorously in fierce denouncing shouts until she could bear it no longer. Half-undressed and with her hair wild, she showed herself at the window, her hands tearing at her clothes.

'Good people! Good people!' she cried. 'Either satisfy your hatred and cruelty by taking my miserable life, or relieve me from the hands of these infamous and inhuman traitors.'

As the people stared up at that distraught quaking face, walled in by stone, looking down at them from the tall house, something moved in them older than Protestanism, the same thing that had made their fathers troop to fight a lost battle for the sake of a man with eyes and brows like hers and impoverish themselves for ransom of another with the same russet hair as she had.

Shouts died away as they stood gazing up at her. What was their Queen doing yonder, half-clothed, appealing and beseeching from a room like a prison when by rights she should be governing and graciously commanding in Holyrood, and they on their knees before her?

A tall man with high shoulders passed below her window— Maitland of Lethington, who was known as Mitchell Wylie (Machiavelli) on the causeways of Edinburgh. They heard her call to him for the love of God to come and speak with her, but he pulled his hat over his face and, without looking up, would have hurried on if the populace, with their hisses and jeers, had not forced him to change his mind and retrace his steps. The Queen's form vanished suddenly from the window as her guards pulled her from it, and the crowd was roughly made to disperse.

We have two accounts of the interview that took place between the man who had been her Secretary of State and his sovereign—Lethington's and Mary's (speaking through her French secretary Nau). It is too much to expect with two such strongly entrenched protagonists that their accounts will dovetail, but they are not incompatible; and there are details in Mary's which fill in and probably give a truer picture of what was said that day in the room fronting the noisy street.

Her version is that of the female at bay relentlessly trying to pin down the hedging, reluctant male. She remembered to tell Nau that Lethington was in such shame and fear he never dared lift his eyes to her face while he spoke to her. He evinced great hatred of Bothwell (no news to Mary), and told her she could not be allowed to return to him. (We can hear Lethington's voice off stage accusing Bothwell of the King's murder.) Mary marvelled at his impudence, and said she was ready to join in the pursuit of Darnley's murderers—the chief reason why the inquiry had not been proceeded with in the past was because he, Morton and Balfour had prevented it. Mary knew why—Bothwell had told her they were the culprits and shown her their signatures on the murder bond. She reminded Lethington she had saved his life. If he persecuted her, she would tell what she knew of him. Angrily he replied that she would drive him to extremities to save his life, whereas, if matters were allowed to grow quiet, he might one day be of service to her. His departure was like a retreat, which he covered by telling her the lords would become suspicious and her life be in peril if she kept him talking like this. Mary, whatever her faults, was of heroic mould; Lethington was not.

Lethington's story is that Mary accused him of being extreme against her. She complained of the wrong done by separating her from her husband with whom she had thought to live and die with all the contentment in the world. He replied that instead of doing her a displeasure, they considered it the greatest service and honour they could pay her. Bothwell could not be a husband to her since he had but lately married the Earl of Huntly's sister; he had never really separated from his lawful spouse, and had recently written to her that he held her for his wife and the Queen for his mistress.

It is most improbable Bothwell put such a remark on paper, particularly when the events of the month in which he had been married to Mary can have left him little time for private letter writing. Lethington must either have been repeating gossip or fabricating it, in his effort to blacken her consort in the Queen's eyes.

Mary refused to believe a word of it, and clamoured to be put into a boat with Bothwell and carried whither fortune chose to take them. According to Lethington, his solace was that the lords were ready to do everything she wanted if she would show herself of an amicable temper towards them and abandon my Lord Bothwell.

Morton and one or two of the other lords visited Mary after Lethington but found her 'inconsolable'. They were hard put to it to know what was to be done now and agreed amongst themselves to sign a warrant for her sequestration. This was a major constitutional step to take which they justified by the Queen's refusal to abandon Bothwell. To prove their words, they spoke of an intercepted letter which they said she wrote that day to her lover, calling him her dear heart and promising to rejoin him as soon as she could. Even Mary's resourcefulness could not conjure forth writing materials in a closely guarded room she was not allowed to leave, and the letter was likely a fiction on the part of the lords to placate Grange. He had given his word that they would obey and reverence her as their sovereign, and considered himself dishonoured when she was treated as a prisoner.

As for Mary, the memory of Bothwell must have risen like a tower out of the chaos she saw around her. They wanted her to abandon him who had stood so stoutly by her when Davie was murdered, and it must be remembered she was now in the hands of the men who had murdered her Italian servant. They wanted her to forget him who was as a part of herself. They wanted her to renounce and denounce him for whom she would relin-

quish both crown and kingdom. Never would she consent that
he should fare worse or have more harm than herself.

That evening she was taken to Holyrood to appease one part
of the populace which had begun to mutter and question, but,
to gratify the over-zealous Protestants, the painted banner was
borne before her. She rode quietly enough beside Morton, for
she thought she was to be reinstated in her palace.

She was followed by two of her Maries and a few members
of her household, mostly Frenchwomen. Mary Seton had accompanied her from Carberry Hill but was only now permitted near
her, and Mary Livingstone was ready to attend her although her
father-in-law had signed the warrant for the Queen's imprisonment. Her train of women kept very close to her, for the short
distance between the Black Turnpike and Holyrood was made
long and hideous by the cries of 'Burn her!' 'Drown her!' Mary
was no longer piteous or pitiable. 'I am innocent', she cried again
and again to her people, 'I have done nothing worthy of blame.
Why am I handled thus, seeing I am a true Princess and your
native Sovereign?'

The place chosen for her imprisonment was the Castle of
Lochleven, because it was on a lonely island more than a mile
from shore and its laird, a Douglas, deemed a fit gaoler for a
recalcitrant Stewart Queen. He was Sir William Douglas, close
kin to Morton and half-brother of Moray. Its chatelaine was
Moray's and the Laird's mother, who, in the short swift years of
her youth, had been mistress of his and Mary's father, James V.

That night Mary was taken alone from her ill-fated palace of
Holyrood which she was never again to enter. She managed to
send a message through one of her ladies to Sir James Balfour,
the Keeper of Edinburgh Castle, entreating him to be loyal to
her and hold it for her, but already he had made his peace with
the enemy lords. Between Lindsay and Ruthven, with a guard
of soldiers, she was hurried past shuttered windows and bolted

doors that she might be carried to her prison by night as the uncertain populace slept. In vain, when they came to open country, she reined back her horse in the frantic hope that Huntly or the Hamiltons would ride out of the dark to her rescue. When they reached the lochside, she refused to enter the boat waiting to convey her to the island, and had to be lifted into it.

For fifteen days she lay, the wavering murmur of water her background, without eating, drinking or speaking. But she did not die as many thought she would. Memories must have scattered through her mind as she lay there, like leaves blown by a fitful gust of wind; and each day that passed she, with laborious patience, would strengthen and prepare herself to bear the story they would tell once they were all linked together. When she was able to rise and go to the narrow window, walking carefully as one walks after a long illness, as though she were uncertain of the very floor she trod upon, she saw, across a stretch of water, low hills and expanses of dreary whinny-muirs bound the distance.

Mary was to say she had in black and white that which could hang Lethington by the neck. This was not the bond Bothwell gave her at Carberry Hill: it is believed to have been taken from her in captivity and burnt with certain other writings which exposed her enemies. They 'kept to be shown' only that which incriminated her.

Two days after she had been taken to Lochleven a small silver casket covered with green velvet, which had been in Bothwell's possession, fell into the lords' hands. It was broken open and said to contain letters and sonnets written by the Queen to Bothwell.

It is unnecessary to wonder here if the letters produced later in evidence against the Queen were identical with the originals. The important point to bear in mind is that, with the opening of the casket, Mary's enemies held 'new cards, genuine or packed', which they could play when and as they chose.

Her gaolers, who alone were allowed access to her, reported that the Queen, after some weeks of her imprisonment, was calmed and better quieted than of late, taking both rest and meat. They said she went in great fear of her life. Mary knew the Protestant clergy, inflamed by Master Knox who was now returned to his country, were calling for her blood; she knew her people were demanding that she be burnt as the murderess of her husband, and the horror of the stake tortured her waking moments and filled her nights with terror.

She was rigorously guarded and complained bitterly of her harsh treatment. She told those about her she would be well content to live in a nunnery in France, or with her grandmother, the old Dowager of Guise. She requested the lords to think of her health and remove her to Stirling, where she could have the comfort and company of her son. She asked, if they would not change her from Lochleven, to allow her gentlewomen to join her, her apothecary, a valet and a needlewoman to prepare embroidery for her to sew. Nothing would induce her to divorce Bothwell, whom the lords had now outlawed and were trying to capture—she would rather die than that, for she was pregnant and divorce would destroy the legitimacy of their child.

The lords would have preferred to take the life of the inopportune Queen on their hands, and thus free themselves of her once and for all. What debarred them was the fear that her death might give France and/or England an excuse to invade Scotland. For Elizabeth, but not her ministers, had come down roundly on Mary's side.

The English Queen belonged to the most exclusive guild in the world, that of crowned heads, which did not admit the right of subjects to attempt anything against the sacred person of their sovereign. She sent an ambassador to Scotland to console and promise help to her imprisoned sister Queen; although he was not permitted to see her, he was convinced his presence saved her life.

Since she refused to divorce Bothwell, the lords determined to compel her to abdicate the throne in favour of her son. Lindsay arrived at Lochleven in boasting mood with Ruthven, two notaries, Robert Melville—who, like his lively brother James had the Queen's interests at heart—and three deeds for her to sign.

Mary was ill, the result of a miscarriage. Her very femininity, her imprecations, even her pathos, drew out all that was sadistic and destructive in certain men, and it had this effect on Patrick Lindsay. He made it plain that if she did not sign, secret execution awaited her who already went in dread of public trial. The Laird of Lochleven refused to be present at this scene taking place under his roof, and his younger brother George, so good-looking he was known as Bonnie Geordie, indignantly remonstrated with his brother-in-law Lindsay for his savageness.

Thus Mary abdicated, resigning, on account of broken health and spirits, the government of the country to her baby son. Robert Melville, in the name of Lethington, Grange and others, advised her to submit as her signature meant nothing while she was held prisoner. But it was a sorry thing to sign away one's queendom even for a moment, to save one's life and evade trial.

A few days after she had subscribed the act of abdication, she heard cannon shot, and loud acclamation and shouts of jubilation rang throughout the castle and its courtyards. It must have seemed strange to listen to such glad rejoicing in a world that for her was sterile and desolate, bereft of all joy. When she asked what event was being so unstintingly celebrated, she was told to make merry as that day the infant Prince was crowned King of Scots.

Her half-brother had now been named as Regent, and hurried home from France via England. He saw as little as he could of his cousin Elizabeth when he was in London, since she was waspish with vituperation against the Scots lords whose 'usage and proceedings against their sovereign lady and Queen overpasses all.' He gave out that he was not at all sure whether or not he would accept the government of his country, but those of his company noticed he was right glad when he first heard he was named Regent.

It was not until evening that the brother and sister were alone together on his first visit to her at Lochleven. Mary always said more to him than she meant, for his quietness made her feel she must not allow a pause to fall between her and this reserved, watching man, who often left her with the uneasy feeling that he had learnt much from her and she nothing about him.

Now she engulfed him with passionate complaint. She is said to have opposed his acceptance of the Regency, which explains his attitude towards her in this interview. Finding her protestations failed to break through his barrier of silence, she began to ply him with eager questions which abated into those full of fear. Still he remained silent until she implored him to speak to her.

Thus invited, he began, detailing step by step the events of her life in the past two years like a prosecuting attorney or a 'ghostly father'. 'Sometimes the Queen wept, sometimes she admitted her inadvisedness and misgovernment, some things she did confess plainly, some things she did excuse, some things she did extenuate.' At one o'clock he left her with hope of nothing but God's mercy, and she spent the night in an agony of fear.

Early next morning she sent for her brother and now it was she who pressed him to accept the Regency, he who declared many reasons why he should refuse it. But at length she prevailed on him to overcome his reluctance. He assured her of her life, but said it did not lie in his power to grant her liberty, nor was it good for her to have it at present. He warned her what would endanger her life: if she attempted to escape, to stir up trouble either in or outside the realm (soliciting help from France or England), and persisted in her inordinate affection for the Earl of Bothwell. Lastly she must have no revengeful thoughts towards these lords and others who had sought her 'reformation and preservation'. We are told Mary took him in her arms and kissed him, but the injuries he had done her with his recriminations 'cut the thread of love and credit betwixt the Queen and him for ever.'

Perhaps to conciliate her brother still further, Mary's ardent temperament made her tend to paint the lily. Mary entrusted her private jewels to him—perhaps she may have thought they would be safest in his keeping. Some he sold, others he gave to his wife. The collection included his sister's famous pearls brought from France, twenty-five of which were the colour of and as large as black grapes. For these Catherine de Medici was prepared to pay their value, but Moray gave them to Elizabeth at bargain price.

Understandably enough, Moray, before he left the island, told the Laird, Lindsay and Ruthven, in Mary's presence, that they were to treat her with gentleness and grant her all the liberty they could. The conditions of her imprisonment ameliorated somewhat, but it was hoped to weary her into renouncing Bothwell, who had escaped to Denmark.

Mary Seton was allowed to join her, and two maids. Nothing reached her that was not scrutinised and sanctioned by her careful brother, and she was not allowed to draw on her costly and extensive wardrobe. He permitted six of her own pocket-handkerchiefs, embroidered and fringed with gold, to be taken to her, and she was able to obtain different colours of silks, some hanks of gold and silver thread for her needlework. It was probably her embroidery that kept her sane. Using needle instead of brush, she made pictures symbolising the story of her wrongs, and the cruelty of a merciless enemy. The tapestry is still in existence, not quite finished, just as she left it when she made her escape.

Her presence began to permeate the castle. Sometimes the Laird took her on the loch in a boat. He was heard to mention to those in authority that in his opinion his prisoner had been punished enough and should be restored to the throne. 'There runs no vice in her but that the same is as largely in you,' he remarked to his kinsman Morton, 'except that your Grace descended not to the destruction of your wife,' he added more lugubriously than hurriedly. His younger brother George became so enamoured of their official guest that soon his distracted love for her was the talk of the whole household. A small sixteen-year-old-page, a foundling dependant on the Laird, was not in an exalted enough position to be noticed except by the Queen. She called Willie Douglas 'my little friend.'

Her brother when he visited her again reported in his ambiguous way that she was as merry and wanton as at any time since she was detained. Mary took this opportunity to complain to him that George Douglas's passion insulted her, whereupon Moray had his half-brother sent from the island in disgrace. Perhaps if he had witnessed his sister bidding handsome George Douglas good-bye he would not have thought the farewell that of an injured woman to the man who had insulted her. It must have been more like the parting of ardent plotters who hope to greet one another soon again.

Mary had promise of aid sent secretly to her from the unstable Hamiltons and Huntly; she could depend on the loyalty of Lord Fleming and Lord Seton, of Livingstone, Herries and Crawford; she received privily a token of goodwill from Lethington; and a ring with a letter of endearment and sympathy, promising help, from Queen Elizabeth. While the Queen of Spain, little berry-brown Madame Ysabel of far-off days in France, tried to make her peace with the Roman Catholics alienated by her Protestant marriage, assuring the Nuncio in Madrid that her one-time play-mate had acknowledged her fault and become Catholic and spiritual again.

The Hamiltons, bitter enemies of the Regent, were wishful to restore Mary to the throne that she might marry one of their sons. Catholic Huntly had to pin his flag to a broken mast and pray for the best. Lethington dared not be too obdurate against her because of her knowledge of his part in the King's murder. George Douglas had himself banished from the island that he might be of more use on shore to her whom he hoped to betroth when he effected her escape. But little Willie Douglas would gladly have laid down his life for her without thought of reward and counted himself fortunate to die for so sweet a cause.

The pitiless blue sky of summer changed into the angry sky of autumn, with dark clouds jealously banking back the rays of the weakening sun; the livid sky of autumn merged into the low-hung sky of winter, and mists wrapped in upon itself the castle on the island. Light faded from the earth, leaving a winter-weary landscape. The blurred moon looked down on a ghostly world inhabited by trees stark as though their scared spirits had long since fled. Now shouldering winds gathered from every corner of the world to assault this hidden place, until the air was filled with the creaking and bluster of sound, and the voice of the loch swelled into that of the sea.

The castle was damp; when the waters rose they washed the cellars of the old tower. Once as Mary was watching the monotonous waves, mounting only to break into nothingness, she thought that her life was now as they, futile and unsubstantial. The idea took possession of her that she, denied the freedom of earth and air, had water all round her, and how swiftly she could end it all. But religion had taught her to look upon even the thought of suicide as sin, and she prayed that she might remember there was no prison for a soul enfranchised by God.

She was not allowed pen or paper. The few letters she managed to write were with materials smuggled to her by inmates of the castle at grave risk both to herself and them. She wrote to Catherine de Medici in France, beseeching her to have compassion on her wretched condition and send troops to deliver her, when Mary assured her mother-in-law great numbers of her subjects would rise to join them.

The snow began to melt on the mainland and restless spring stirred in the sap of trees. Mary made an abortive attempt to escape, and her restraint was tightened in consequence.

But one day a pearl ear-ring was pressed into her hand as a sign that George Douglas had everything in readiness on shore. That evening a hooded woman in a peasant's kirtle with her child (a ten-year-old serving-maid) crossed the castle courtyard as the Laird and his household sat at supper. They met the foundling Willie, who opened the gate for them with the only keys belonging to the Laird himself, and all three passed without. The gate was locked by Willie on the outside that no one could come after them, and the Queen and her maid followed him to an unfastened boat.

It lay beside others, all of whose chains he had tampered with during the day to make them difficult to unloosen should they be pursued. His companions entered the boat which he pushed from the shingly shore before leaping in after them. Mary hid herself under the steersman's seat as Willie grasped the oars. Halfway over the loch he paused to throw the keys of the castle into the loch, crying out to the Queen, 'To the kelpies' keeping!'

She was sitting on the seat now, waving a white veil as a signal that it was she in the boat. When it grounded on shore, George Douglas was there to lift her from it.

She was drunken with the joy of freedom, but she would not

mount her horse till Willie Douglas was safely on his. Guarded with a troop of horsemen, they rode through the night towards Niddrie Castle. Twice on the way they were stopped by low challenging voices which praised God when they learnt that the Queen was with them. Once it was Lord Seton, to whose castle they were journeying, and later Lord Claud Hamilton, both with companies of men.

When Niddrie Castle was reached, Mary could neither sleep nor rest. She spent the hours of early morning writing to her uncle, the Cardinal of Lorraine, to announce, by the grace of God, her escape, and instructing a kinsman of Bothwell's first to seize the Castle of Dunbar and then to bear the glad news of her release to his chief in Denmark.

Long before sunrise, the heartening notes of pipes and bugles sounded as Livingstones, Bruces and other nobles rode up to prove their loyalty with men.

In her excitement Mary did not wait for her hair to be dressed but, with it streaming behind her in all its brightness, appeared at a broad window to thank them for their love. The picture is caught for us to remember before that face, with the shine of a May morning upon it, is made terrible with suffering.

BOOK FOUR
Winter
May 1568 – February 1587

CHAPTER ONE

We're a' here Queen Mary's men;
And we've come here to crave our right.

On the third of May a messenger rode breathlessly to the
Regent, holding a justice court in Glasgow, to acquaint
him with the unwelcome news that the Queen had escaped from
Lochleven the previous night. We read that Moray was sore
amazed by these unlooked-for tidings. He had only a small bodyguard with him, but at once called the confederate lords to his
aid and issued a proclamation summoning troops in the King's
name. Grange brought the garrison of Edinburgh Castle, Morton came with men and money, and Glasgow itself, a Lennox
stronghold, provided a large contingent.

But those who rallied to him were not so considerable as those
who rallied to his sister. Never, a Frenchman remarked of her
forces, had he seen so many men so suddenly convened; they
sprang up as though by magic. The Regent was proving himself
an able indefatigable ruler, and ability to keep order in these
days called for a ruthless hand. Many of those who now joined
Mary were reactionaries from his authority. She had Protestant
as well as Catholic personal friends: Herries, Seton, Fleming,
Livingstone; her brother-in-law Argyle brought Highland forces
to fight on her behalf, and above all there were the Hamiltons.

They had been willing enough for her to be put to death after
Carberry, as that left only a weak infant between them and their
claim to the throne, but when her half-brother was made Regent,
her cause became theirs and they connived at her escape from

Lochleven. Now with the Queen no longer a prisoner but free to be married to Lord John Hamilton, they saw at dizzy last the triumph of their house within their grasp.

The Castle of Dumbarton was in their hands, from where Mary could sail to France if the tide of battle turned against her. But no Hamilton thought of such an eventuality in these crowded days of early May, and she was carried instead to Hamilton, some miles from Glasgow, which was more favourable to convene men than Dumbarton Castle standing solitary on its rock in the river Clyde.

From here Mary's abdication was pronounced null and void, having been extorted from her by fear. A copy of this pronouncement was sent to Moray and his confederates, requiring them to restore her peacefully to her royal dignity and estate and promising that, if they would comply with her just demand, she would remit and forgive all they had done against her person and honour. Both sides knew there was no hope of restoration or restitution on these lines. Moray played for time as he took businesslike measures to guard what he held, and Mary wrote urgently to France praying for a thousand troops to be sent for her immediate need.

Her wisest procedure, after her escape from Lochleven, would undoubtedly have been to make for the safe stronghold of Dumbarton Castle, and try to draw home to herself little by little the allegiance of her subjects. That is probably what she would have chosen had the decision been hers, but the Hamiltons had other plans. Their superior numbers gave them soaring confidence, and they wanted instant battle with the man they hated most, the base-born Moray, who had so long held their house in check.

The Regent, joined by his partisans, was advised to fall back on Stirling, but he knew his strong-arm methods had not gained him popularity, and that if he appeared intimidated the country would rise and declare itself for the Queen. He therefore re-

mained where he was, to bar if he could his sister's approach to
Dumbarton and win the day before her full strength had time
to gather or consolidate. And the heady Hamiltons played into
his hands.

Between her escape from Lochleven and the battle of Langside lay ten days packed with ever mounting excitement as she
issued counterblasts to her brother's proclamations and tried to
bring some concord amongst her ever increasing forces. Most of
her chiefs appeared more taken up with their enmity to each
other than the common foe, and there were rankling disputes
about precedency. Lord Herries was the ablest man on her side,
but feckless Argyle was made commander mainly because he had
brought most men. Even the elements conspired against Mary.
Because of unprecedented rainfall, Highland rivers were made
impassable and Huntly could not reach her in time.

But everything looked auspicious for her on that beautiful
spring day, the 13th May, and her heart and hopes rode high.
Maxwell, a near kinsman of Darnley's, joined her with his vassals
and tenants on the very morning of battle, and she knighted him
below the royal standard, the last honour she was to bestow.

The Regent's party had not numbers but was compact, with
a common purpose, and Moray a tried general. He ordered every
one of his horsemen to take up a foot-soldier behind him and
thus had the village of Langside occupied with hackbuteers (old-
fashioned musketry). He himself was in command, with Morton
in charge of the rear, while the experienced Grange was strate-
gically placed to watch how the battle fared, that he might re-
inforce when and where needful.

Confident in their numbers, the Hamiltons attacked, pressing
forward to storm the village, while Herries followed with his
Border horsemen to support them in the vauntguard. They
gained ground with the charge and valiantly raised every effort
to maintain it, while they waited for Argyle to bring up the main

army. But no aid came from Argyle who, seized by a fit in the midst of battle, was incapable of giving the smallest command, and his Highland forces broke up in wild confusion. Grange rushed his pikemen to help the hackbuteers, and the Hamiltons and Herries were driven back under the arrow-rain of the bowmen and the fire of the musketry, against the routed, fleeing Highlanders.

Moray's victory was practically bloodless; he lost two men. The numbers killed on the Queen's side ran into hundreds, mostly Hamiltons, and there would have been butchery had the Regent and Grange not taken personal steps to forbid it. Many prisoners were captured, again mostly Hamiltons. The lives of some of the lairds were spared, but their estates were sequestrated.

From a high knoll, Mary witnessed her battle lost with incredible, fearful swiftness, under an hour. Her last hope lay in reaching Dumbarton Castle and with a handful of followers she hastened towards the Clyde. But this was Lennox country and there is a sinister story that when she and Lord Herries were about to reach the river, two men, working in the fields, menaced them with their scythes and they had to turn back.

She was so hotly pursued that she had not time to take the boat which would bear her to safety. Her company divided to delude the pursuers, and with Herries and his son she made for the moors of the south-west, never drawing rein until she reached Sanquhar. There Mary Seton is said to have cut off the Queen's copper hair to disguise her and, remounting at nightfall to escape detection, they made for Herries's fortified House of Corra. There were no roads, but the father and son knew the unfrequented passes which led into their own trackless country, the wild district of Galloway, whose isolated people still adhered to the old faith.

Melville tells us that 'after the loss of the battle, her Majesty

lost all courage, which she had never done before.' Her greatest
terror was that of falling into her brother's or her subjects'
power. Her predicament was appalling, and the only refuge she
could see for herself was England. Against his will, she made
Herries write to the Deputy-Governor of Carlisle to enquire if
his mistress, the Scots Queen, would be allowed a safe retreat
should she cross the Border. Mary did not wait for his reply,
which by its very guardedness might well have given her pause.

She spent only a few hours at Corra House and before daybreak was on her way to Terregles. Amongst these forsaken
Galloway hills, her ancestor Robert the Bruce had been hunted
as she now was, and her spirits seem to have revived. Why could
she not triumph as he had done despite seemingly invincible
enemies? Buttressed by her small company of friends, she felt
fortified and England faded as her only route of escape.

In a letter she was to write to her uncle, the Cardinal of Lorraine, she describes in her own words something of what she
went through during these harried, haunted days: 'I have suffered injuries, calumnies, captivity, hunger, cold, heat, flying—
without knowing whither—fourscore and twenty miles across
the country without once pausing to alight, and then lay on the
hard ground, having only sour milk to drink, and oatmeal to
eat, without bread, passing three nights like the owls.' Her French
mother-in-law was to wonder that anyone so delicate and tender
as Mary Stewart had been all her life could survive such hard-
ships.

She dared only travel by night and it was dark when she left
Terregles, which was like an outpost receiving diminishing con-
tacts from the known world and with the unknown pressing over
its very doorstep. This was a barren region, whose bald mounded
hills were like the waves of a static sea. When the early hours
of the morning were still chill and numb with night, Lord Herries pointed out to her in the greying distance a hunting-lodge,

telling her it belonged to Bothwell. At the sound of that name, Mary burst into tears.

Some of her adherents brought news that Moray was making preparations to march into Galloway. That decided his sister: at once she determined to change her course and, instead of fleeing into the fastness of Scotland's hinterland, she turned south.

They crossed the Dee at its narrowest, and so alarmed was her escort at the rumour of pursuit they broke down the ancient bridge after use. Mary went into a cottage as they worked at their task, and the woman, unaware of her identity, put before her all she had, probably the oatmeal and sour milk she mentioned in her letter to her uncle. For over two centuries, until the croft became a ruin, the widow and her descendants paid no rent because the Herries family remembered the wish of a fleeing Queen who had partaken hospitality under that roof.

At dawn they reached Kenmure Castle where she rested during the day. Moray razed the building to the ground a month later because it had sheltered his sister. Learning that Archbishop Hamilton and other fugitives from Langside had reached Dundrennan Abbey, the Queen and her party repaired to it. She spent her last night in Scotland at the home of relatives of Lord Herries, and asked that the baby son of her host might share her bed with her.

Traces of her precipitate flight have become embedded in place-names, starting at Crossmyloof where she is reported to have watched her battle being lost with a crucifix in her hand (loof), a wynd where she is said to have been nearly pulled from her horse, the spring where she quenched her thirst, the hill where she rested in a cottage. And in the wake of her flight are scattered possessions, keepsakes of memory: the oaken bedstead where she slept for a few hours in the House of Corra, a rich damask table-cloth with the royal arms she left behind as a gift, and a little ruby ring for her small bedmate.

At Dundrennan Abbey, whose name was like the echo of all
the empty, crying winds that fretted the dreary moors, she had
the agony of learning that fifty-seven lairds of the name of
Hamilton alone had been killed at Langside, with many other
of her bravest friends. Lord Seton, whose loyalty to her had ever
chimed with her hour of need, was dangerously wounded and a
prisoner, he whom she had enshrined in an extempore couplet
written off gaily in Latin and in French:

'Though earls, and dukes, and even kings there be,
    Yet Seton's noble lord sufficeth me.'

It was Sunday, and in Dundrennan Abbey Mary held her last
Council. One and all of those around her pled with, advised
and entreated her not to throw herself on Elizabeth's mercy by
entering England. Herries vouched he could secure her safety
in Galloway for at least forty days, until she found some other
way of escape or until her friends could rally their forces. Others
backed him, suggesting she should retire to one of the strong
fortresses in the neighbourhood, but Mary cried out at them
that it was impossible for her to remain safely in any part of her
realm, not knowing whom to trust. When they spoke to her of
her own people, she remembered those who had stood, screech-
ing and hating, at their doors and windows as she was thrust
past them. She thought of her relentless brother, implacable
Lindsay, Morton with his cruel pin-head eyes.

Some urged her to flee to France. 'I shall never return to
France as a fugitive,' she told them, 'without a retinue, into a
country where I have worn the crown-matrimonial.'

To her there was no alternative to England. Elizabeth was a
sister sovereign, her cousin, her own flesh and blood. They
pointed out that kinship had not prevented her sister sovereign
from plotting against her, harbouring those who had fled from
her justice, paying gold to further her enemies' plans. If she

could prove herself false and untrue when she was a Queen on her throne, how would she prove herself if, a powerless emigrant, Mary entered her country?

When she reminded them that Elizabeth had promised her aid in her captivity at Lochleven, when she showed them the token-ring her cousin had sent to pledge her sincerity, they reminded her that she had never done anything in the past but promise. Scotland was Mary's own country where she had friends, but England—Had she forgotten what had happened to her ancestor, James I, who had been detained many years in captivity when he entered England in time of peace? Their mistress was imaging to herself how she would entertain her cousin if she fled from her country; she was mirroring in the Queen of England her own self whose only faults were those of over-bounty. But the Queen of England was not as she; even those nearest her did not trust her.

But all they said to Mary fell on Stewart ears; her last decree in Scotland was to command her best friends to allow her to have her own way.

From Dundrennan, where she could see England green as the Promised Land across the deceptively shining Solway, Mary wrote to her cousin, returning to her the token-ring. 'By unexpected means, the Almighty Disposer of all things delivered me from the cruel imprisonment I underwent; but I have since lost a battle, in which most of those who preserved their loyal integrity fell before my eyes. I am now forced out of my kingdom, and driven to such straits that, next to God, I have no hope but in your goodness. I beseech you, therefore, my dearest sister, that I may be conducted to your presence, that I may acquaint you with all my affairs. In the meantime, I beseech God to grant you all heavenly benedictions, and to me patience and consolation, which last I hope and pray to obtain by your means. To remind you of the reasons I have to depend on England, I send back to its Queen this token, the jewel of her promised friendship and assistance. Your affectionate sister, M.R.'

Those who determined to accompany her were prompted more by love than by the thought they dare not be left behind; some sixteen people in all including Herries, Fleming, Lord and Lady Livingstone, and the two Douglases, Bonnie Geordie and Foundling Willie. The others went with her to the shore, their voices clamorous with importunity as they continued to strive with her not to embark. No one had made any preparation for such a voyage and the only vessel that could be procured was an ordinary fishing-boat with four men to man it. The Solway was treacherous for such small craft, even in the fine weather of that calm sunny day.

Everything looked bright and fair, intense with the thrust of spring growth. It was exactly a year and a day since she had married Bothwell. The tide served, and the last sovereign of the old house of Stewart entered the rocking, rough boat that was to bear her forever from her native land.

As it moved from the shore, some premonition took possession of Archbishop Hamilton, who rushed into the water and tried to pull it back. But it was dragged out of his powerless hands, and those on the bank watched it draw from them until they could no longer distinguish the darkening figures it carried over the widening firth.

CHAPTER TWO

Sudden the tapers cease to burn,
The minstrels cease to play.

Once they were at sea, when the rugged rocky shore of Scotland had been blurred into that of contour, Mary changed her mind. She wanted to go to France, not England; and in obedience to her wishes, the boatsmen tried to alter their course, but by that time both wind and tide were too strong for them. The craft was driven and pulled swiftly across the firth into the harbour of a small English seafaring town on the Cumberland coast—the voyage took some four hours.

It was Sunday, when England, like Scotland, was on holiday. Onlookers gathered on the southern shore of the Solway to watch curiously the vessel bearing precipitately towards them. Mary was recognised as the Scots Queen whenever she alighted because of her unusual height for a woman and from her profile on her country's coinage. The warmth and demonstration of her welcome must have comforted and cheered her, as the chief noble of the district hospitably conducted her to his pleasant mansion.

From here Mary wrote to Elizabeth, entreating her to send for her as soon as possible, for she was in a pitiable condition, not only for a Queen but even for a gentlewoman, having nothing in the world but the clothes in which she had fled from Scotland. She signed this letter, 'Your very faithful and affectionate good sister and cousin and escaped prisoner, Maria R.'

She was only allowed to remain one night with her generous

host. The English authorities had been alerted to her possible arrival by Lord Herries's earlier letter and the news of her coming spread with inconceivable rapidity. A warrant from the English sovereign ordered the sheriff, magistrates and gentlemen of Cumberland to use the Scottish Queen and her company honourably, but in this letter appears the significant sentence, 'Let none of them escape.'

Elizabeth had reigned for some nine years when Mary entered her country. She was thirty-four now, and her lumpy, sensual body had begun to take on the angular lines familiar from her later portraits. Her small eyes were wary above high cheekbones, and already the face in which they moved was informed with a growing confidence.

For Mary to throw herself on her cousin's mercy was fatal from her point of view, but Elizabeth and England's point of view has also to be taken into account. Cecil, like his sovereign, did not weigh the rights and wrongs of keeping the Scots Queen prisoner. What was best for England justified in their eyes every and any expedient. And Mary could not be allowed to repair to France, where she would have been a constant threat to Elizabeth. Nor could she be permitted even limited freedom as a private individual in England, where her presence would have formed all the support needful for Roman Catholic aspirations. Nor could she in safety be returned to Scotland with Elizabeth's help, where she could involve both countries in the religious wars that were trailing their devastation across the Continent. Hence all the convolutions of Elizabeth's dissembling mind, the subtleties and stratagems of Cecil's intricate policies, can be traced back to the same source—Let not the Scots Queen escape. The shiftings, the plausibilities, the double dealing to lend a semblance of legality, the cruel cat-and-mouse proceedings, can in some measure be explained by the fact that England was balancing precariously on the horns of a dilemma as she tried

to avoid bringing in France or Spain against her in Mary's defence.

We now know that nothing could have been worse for Mary
than the nineteen years of imprisonment she endured in England, but one wonders what her fate would have been had she
arrived in France where her mother-in-law, who had always
hated her, was now the power behind the throne. Again, what
hope lay for her had she returned to Scotland—there was no
possible *modus vivendi* to bridge the distance between her and
her restoration, and had she returned with foreign troops her
people would have fought as they had fought in the past when
their independence was threatened, 'like brute beasts'.

As she eloquently poured the rights of her cause and the
wrongs of her enemies into the sympathetic ears of the many
English squires who flocked from the neighbouring counties to
hear her, Mary was unaware that her predicament had become
like a spider's web: the more she struggled to free herself from
it, the more hopelessly she found herself entrapped.

This countryside was lusher, smoother, gentler, than her native Scotland. She saw it as she was moved from hall to castle:
luxuriant meads watered by the placid Eden which was quite
unlike the turbulent spumy rivers of the north. Little by little
she was borne deeper and deeper into England, farther and farther from the friendly Border where, in the stir of her arrival,
she had held impromptu courts. The procession of men who
were to accompany her throughout her sojourn in her cousin's
realm had already begun to form—her gaolers, courtly Lowther,
punctilious Scrope, stout Bowes, charmed Knollys.

It was Lord Scrope and Sir Francis Knollys who had to deliver
to her Elizabeth's answer to her plea for clothes: two well-worn
shifts, two pairs of shoes and two fragments of black velvet. That
was the gift of one queen to another; Elizabeth would certainly
have had cloth of state from Mary. The bearers felt the insult

so keenly that the Scots Queen, for their sakes, pretended to believe their embarrassed excuses.

Many of her Scots servants, both men and women, repaired to her at Carlisle, but the one Mary was most glad to see was her lady-in-waiting, Mary Seton. She told Knollys that Seton was the finest dresser of hair to be found in any country, and each day his admiring gaze saw a different curled periwig or some new device of head-dressing, 'without any cost', that set forth the Scots Queen 'gaily well'.

It was Knollys who wrote to Cecil of Mary: 'This lady and princess is a notable woman, and seems to regard no ceremonious honour except the acknowledging of her estate royal. She shows a disposition to speak much, to be bold, to be pleasant, and to be very familiar. She shows a great desire to be avenged of her enemies. She shows a readiness to expose herself to all perils, in hope of victory. She desires much to hear of hardiness and valiancy, and commends by name all approved hardy men of her own country, although they be her enemies, and she conceals no cowardice even in her friends. The thing that most she thirsts after is victory, and it seems indifferent to her to have her enemies diminished either by the sword of her friends, by liberal provision and rewards of her purse, or by divisions and quarrels raised among themselves. So that for victory's sake, pain and peril seem pleasant to her; and in respect of victory, wealth and all things seem to her contemptuous and vile.' Well might Knollys conclude, 'Now what is to be done with such a lady and princess?'

Protesting that she went as a prisoner and not at her own free will Mary was taken from Carlisle, which was too near the helpful Catholic Border, and carried to Bolton in Yorkshire on the pretext that Elizabeth desired to bring her nearer to her.

The midsummer sunshine washed over the green countryside as she rode with her attendants, closely guarded. Voices of peo-

ple followed her like short-breathed whispers when she passed
through the streets of towns. The flat-fronted houses on either
side wore an unfamiliar, incurious look. They were quite unlike
the houses in Edinburgh where one felt doors were opened before the tirling-pin was sounded and eyes watched at windows
before footsteps were heard.

The dwelling at Bolton to which she was taken was a strong,
high-walled castle round which the wind played at night, feeling
at windows, trembling down the long tunnelling chimneys,
sounding at doors, like fingers straying over organ stops. Elizabeth's provision for her enforced guest was so parsimonious that
plenishings to make the castle habitable for its royal inmate had
to be borrowed from various gentry in the neighbourhood. 'I
beseech you to consider my necessity,' Mary wrote to Catherine
de Medici. 'The King owes me money (her dowries), and I
have not one sou! I am not ashamed to address my plaints to
you by whom I was brought up; for I have not the wherewithal
to buy a chemise.'

Although Mary went to bed late, the grudging hours took long
to pass. Her letters vibrate with the horror of what was happening to her loyal followers in Scotland. 'They beat down the
houses of my servants,' she wrote to her Cardinal uncle, 'and I
cannot aid them, and hang the masters of them while I am unable to preserve them.' She made arrangements for George
Douglas to be sent to France out of danger's way; her heart bled
for her 'poor Lord Seton' whom they were threatening to hang
because he had helped her to escape from Lochleven, and she
exhorted her uncle to do everything in his power on his behalf
and that of her other faithful friends.

Little Madame Ysabel, the Queen of Spain, wrote to comfort
her one-time playmate in her distress, and Mary replied with
characteristic gratitude, 'Your letters seemed to be sent by God
for my consolation in the midst of the manifold troubles which

surround me.' When she had asked for a priest in her cousin's
realm, she was met by the curt rejoinder, 'There are no priests
in England.' She told her royal sister-in-law that she would
rather die than forsake the faith in which they had been nurtured
together, and reminded Ysabel of her playful suggestion after
the birth of Mary's son that he should marry one of her little
daughters. Mary wrote it was her ardent wish that what was said
in sport should be brought to pass in good earnest, for such an
alliance might well be the means of re-establishing the ancient
faith both in England and Scotland.

The men she appointed to speak on her behalf were loyal but
had little strength of personality to stamp upon or carry forward
her cause. Ineffectual Bishop Leslie was one, who years ago had
raced to France to invite her to return to Scotland with Catholic
arms. There is a disastrous sentence of Herries which undoes all
his boldness before Elizabeth when he asked the English Queen
what would happen if she came to the conclusion the Scots
Queen was guilty, 'which may God forbid.'

Mary's days passed fitfully, long restless periods of waiting for
her commissioners to return to her alternated with times of
feverish activity when she heard from Queen Elizabeth or news
from Scotland. Her cousin's letters did nothing to ease Mary's
inquietude. In terrible straits, she, blind with trust, had fled to
England to state her plight to a sister sovereign who had promised her succour and who now signified she could not receive
her into her presence until she had cleared herself of the reports
connecting her with her husband's murder. How could one clear
oneself if one were not granted a hearing to explain by confidence, confute with counter-accusation, purge with extenuation?
Was there any woman on earth who would condemn her when
she knew all? And she had meant to reveal all to Elizabeth in
that warm-hearted meeting she had never dreamed of being
denied.

At the Queen of England's board, Mary's thoughts found only stinted food. Elizabeth's sovereign remedy for her cousin's ills was to force her to consent to place her case and that of her brother's party in her hands. Mary might lose her country, be begrudged the allegiance of her people, and divested of the power of a throne, but nothing that ever happened to her could rob her of the belief that she, an anointed Queen, was subject to no judge on earth, to no tribunal but that of God. Since there was no better cure at hand, she agreed that an investigation should take place, not for tribunal—marry! she knew her degree of state better than that—but for Elizabeth's friendly arbitration. And she only agreed thus much on Elizabeth's assurance that, *whatever the investigation yielded,* she should be restored to her seat royal.

As yet the dark blot on her reputation was her marriage to Bothwell. Her connection with the King's murder was based only on dubious hearsay and ready-tongued rumour. But even now, hastening to England to present Queen Elizabeth with their indictment against her, came the Regent's party. It was headed by her half-brother, into whose mind she had never been able to penetrate, and included the heavy, brazen Earl of Morton, and Maitland of Lethington, who deemed it wiser to come to England to attempt a compromise than remain in Scotland. The very mention of his name provoked from Mary a torrent of upbraiding words. Well, brought face to face, she would outbrave them all, prove beyond a doubt that they, her enemies, were attempting to clear themselves or their friends of the King's murder by casting it solely on her. She had sufficient proof in her possession of Lethington's guilt to hang him by the neck.

But her brother, who tested every inch of his way before he took a step, and truculent Morton had not come to England with only windy words and unproven crimination to support them. They had still to use their strongest weapon against her—

the bundle of sonnets and letters, proving her connection with her husband's death, which they said had been written by her to Bothwell in the lost, far-off days of a year ago.

No one but Elizabeth and old, unhappy Lennox was wishful that a full investigation of the King's murder should take place. Each of the other parties was looking for a cupboard in which to hide their skeleton, anxious to let compromise turn the key, particularly the Laird of Lethington, who knew his life lay in Mary's hands. His propitiatory offering was to suppress if he could her brother's accusation of her and stifle her with gratitude by effecting her marriage to the Duke of Norfolk, the most powerful nobleman in England. But the English Queen was resolved to force Moray to do his utmost. She was not going to permit her Catholic rival to pass from her safe keeping to loving hearts and helpful hands in France; nor must she be allowed to return to rule in Scotland; but she could not be held in England without some show of reason. That reason Elizabeth determined to make Moray give her.

With ever-growing mistrust, Mary became aware that Elizabeth's bent for the whole case to be fully stated was not that she, her cousin, might be cleared of charges in which Elizabeth feigned not to believe, but that she might be irreparably besmirched and rendered politically helpless.

When autumn was darkening into winter, and the feeble sun moiled into the murky heavens, when sucking mud and damp leaf mould muffled hooves and choked wheels on the rutted roads, the English commission met. And Mary, four days' distance from the conference, waited.

Even to the end she trusted that a compromise might be effected to save her crown and honour; but if she were accused, she was prepared for her accusers. So great an injustice never occurred to her that she might be accused and yet not permitted to be present to reply.

As she waited she, who never thought of a future happening but she pictured it into a living scene, passed the dreary time enacting in thought the spectacle of herself in the Painted Hall of Westminster discomfiting and silencing her enemies before the peers of England and the foreign ambassadors. When she exposed her accusers as themselves guilty, small faith would be placed in the letters they had in their possession, letters she declared to be forged or garbled. For every question that might be asked her, she had a reply in readiness. She would carry by storm her hearers with the power of her individuality, the appeal of her voice and tears, for she had behind her the conviction and strength of a woman so wronged that she had now come to think of herself as blameless.

The conference lasted for days that dragged into weeks. Her brother, who had agreed to suppress his accusation on certain conditions, nevertheless produced his charge, denouncing his sister as alone devising and commanding her husband's death, which was merely executed by Bothwell. The overlooked, pitifully earnest Earl of Lennox was permitted to appear as prosecutor of his son's wife and certain of his evidence was accepted. Mary's commissioners, realising that the conference was no longer a court of arbitration but a court presumably of law with their mistress as the accused, demanded once again that she be heard personally and admitted, as Moray had been, to Queen Elizabeth's presence. Their protests were in vain, the proceedings were not stayed and the conclusion was arrived at that the Queen of England could not, in view of so vehement allegations and presumptions, agree to have the Queen of Scots come into

James VI of Scotland, later
James I of England, at the
age of eight
By an Unknown Artist
National Portrait Gallery,
London

'No more tears to fall'
By an Artist of the School of Clouet
Condé Museum, Chantilly

Mary at thirty-six
Attributed to P. Oudry
National Portrait Gallery, London

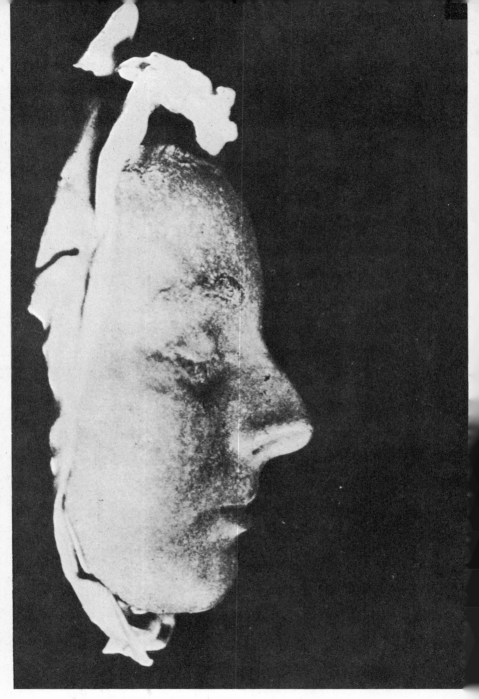

Death Mask of Mary, Queen of Scots, at Holyrood
By courtesy of the Duke of Hamilton

her presence, until the said horrible crimes were removed from her.

It was a winter of unusual severity even for that mountainous Yorkshire district, and the roads were made impassable with snow. Mary, powerless, saw her case weakened and defamed by the fatal temporising of her own commissioners, learnt she was judged unlawfully without a hearing and condemned on evidence she was never permitted to see.

Instead of a haven, England had proved a trap; instead of a protector, Elizabeth had revealed herself a destroyer. Bitter were Mary's troubled thoughts through the faint winter days as the cold grey light from the high window crept imperceptibly across the floor of her room, and her twenty-sixth birthday came and went.

But hope took long to die in so joyous and sanguine a heart. A day would surely dawn and soon when she would see just vengeance flail her enemies. England did not span the universe, Queen Elizabeth did not rule the world. There was the King of Spain and her good brother the King of France, the little Charles of her childhood days, and other Catholic princes and powers who, moved at the ill-treatment meted out to her by Protestant hands, had begun to forget her heretical marriage to a divorced Scots Protestant nobleman. There were, even in Elizabeth's realm, men who were ready to aid her, mighty men like the ambitious Duke of Norfolk, and the headlong Catholic Earls of Northumberland and Westmoreland.

CHAPTER THREE

Their wings are cut and they cannot fly,
Cannot fly, cannot fly,
Their wings are cut and they cannot fly.

IT was gradually borne in on those around the Scots Queen that, despite shifting promises to the contrary, no help for her restoration would come from Queen Elizabeth. Her cousin would unlawfully detain rather than grant liberty to a prisoner whose adherents claimed her to be the rightful sovereign of England.

Mary could scarcely contain her exultation when she heard her half-brother, the Earl of Moray, had been murdered by a Hamilton in the town where she was born. Four shots cracked through the frost-bound air and he had reeled in his saddle. Voices were suddenly hushed as he dismounted from his horse.

A way was made for him through the press of people who had gathered to see the Regent pass by, and he walked to the palace of Linlithgow to die, leaving the straggling grey street empty but for its silent houses standing in each other's shadows.

Tidings of her party's defeats in Scotland were carried hastily to her, while eyes watched greedily how she received and bore up under them. Huntly, who had raised her standard in the north, was forced to submit, and her powerful Castle of Dumbarton, where supplies had been received from France, was sold by a traitor to the enemy. Only the Castle of Edinburgh remained, standing mighty and inviolate upon its rock.

It was held for the Scots Queen by Kirkcaldy of Grange, the

soldier to whom she had surrendered at Carberry and who never forgot he had given his word she would be treated as their sovereign; and by Maitland of Lethington, who died, paradoxically enough, as Mary's man. Shortly before his death, Moray had charged the Secretary, who refused to join him in the betrayal of the Duke of Norfolk, as accessory to the King's murder. But, while awaiting his trial, Lethington had been released by a letter, purporting to be from the Regent, commanding that he be given over to the Captain of Edinburgh Castle, who was his friend and the writer of the letter, Kirkcaldy of Grange. Grange also freed prisoners held in the fortress because of their loyalty to the Queen, including Lord Seton.

Edinburgh Castle was the strongest and the last foothold of Mary's party in Scotland. For three long years it withstood siege, even after its wells had been poisoned. Because he was not able to abide the vibration, the one-time Secretary was placed in a low vault, his legs so paralysed he could not walk, his body so frail he could not endure even to sneeze, his dream of the unity of the two crowns shattered, his mouth no longer whimsical but wry. How long ago since he had written to Cecil that merriness was the best remedy for all diseases.

Artillery was sent from over the Border and it was stormed by the English. The tale of its fall was brought exultingly to Mary. 'You are always a messenger of evil tidings,' she told her gaoler Shrewsbury, 'and never bring me anything good.' He reported to Cecil, 'She makes little show of any grief, yet this news nips her very sore.'

Kirkcaldy, despite the terms of his surrender to the English commander, was handed over to Morton, now Regent, and hanged with his face against the sun that a prophecy of Master Knox's might be fulfilled. Lethington died in prison a few days after the surrender, escaping what he dreaded most—public execution; and his wife, Mary Fleming, one of the Queen's four

Maries, sailed with her children to poverty and exile in France.

Mary had her servants and attendants round her, she was visited perpetually by her guardians, but the rest of the world had slanted from her. She never saw in flesh and blood the men who now came into her life, and they moved into her ken like reflections across a mirror. Although the Scots now refused to sanction her divorce from Bothwell, an accommodating Catholic Bull would pave the way to an advantageous marriage once she was at liberty.

Northumberland and Westmoreland both lost their lives in consequence of an ill-starred precipitate attempt to rescue her, and, for plotting against his country and sovereign, the Duke of Norfolk was beheaded—he to whom she wrote letters promising him her constant submission, like the bloodless shadows of letters she had written in another world to another man. Ah, *he* would not have needed to be bolstered and spurred on as she had to inspirit and instigate this uncertain Norfolk, who no longer had the Laird of Lethington by him to bid him have good cheer and convince him how simple it was all going to be. Shrinking and laggard, death at last determined his mind, and he went with a quiet nobility to the scaffold, her best hope of deliverance gone. He said of the unseen woman he was wooing, 'Nothing that anybody goeth about for her nor that she doeth herself prospereth': it was like her epitaph.

Both English Houses of Parliament, after his execution, petitioned their sovereign that the Scots Queen should share his fate, but Elizabeth replied she could not put to death the bird that had fled to her for succour from the hawk. Touched and moved by her people's loyalty, she could afford to be generous to her rival.

Any popularity Mary had enjoyed in Scotland was fugitive compared to this basic power upon which her cousin could draw. Elizabeth's strength as a ruler was that she could read the mind

of the nation she governed, whereas that of Mary's people was a
closed book to her. The difference of religion separated her from
them as her long absence in France could not have done. From
Mary's day the great body of her countrymen was no longer to
rally round the Stewart standard, the main stream of Scottish
life was to pass it by. It no longer represented them but, flown
for lost causes, a mere segment of the nation.

Through those nineteen dreetling years of captivity, she was
like a bemused bird which, imprisoned in a room, destroys itself by throwing its body against the invisible window-pane in a
maddened attempt to reach the outside it so clearly sees. Plot
after plot was embarked upon, manned with prayer and buoyant
confidence, and plot after plot was discovered. Her apprehended
envoys, threatened with the rack, revealed more than need be;
her household was reduced; she was moved from prison to
prison, and rigorously secluded. Still that greying face could be
seen bending over her letters in the silence of the night as she
wrote in her broken handwriting to prince and king, Queen
Elizabeth and the Pope, to ambassador, emissary and nuncio, to
her kinsmen in France and her son in Scotland. And outside the
world still marched, heedless of her, the world good with earth
and sea and cloud.

Autumn usurped summers, springs loosened winter's unwilling hold, and the child she had left a cradled infant in harried
Scotland grew from a terrorised bairn King into an old young
man who recorded his detestation of Roman Catholics and grew
in political importance every year of his life. The letters she sent
him when he was a little boy, her gifts of ponies and saddles,
never reached him because she could not bring herself to address
him as King.

His world was an insecure place where each man was against
his brother and even one's rights were threatened, a place where
one had to grip what one had in case it were taken from one,

outwit with craft and protect oneself with cunning. The timidity
he suffered from as a child, when he was seized first by one and
then another faction of men all intent to use him for their own
purposes, strengthened as he grew older into an overweening belief in his kingship.

To Mary, this unknown child was the son she had borne, flesh
of her flesh, from whom she looked for love and obedience and
deliverance. To him, she was an unremembered mother whose
name he heard from his earliest years defamed and stigmatised,
whose shame and dishonour he had been burdened with by Kirk
and tutor: an unknown woman who wanted to share his throne
with him, a would-be rival to his power.

She spent hours at a time over her embroidery frame, her fine
fingers working crosses and crowns, lilies and pomegranates,
roses and unicorns, with thread of silver, silks of red, of green and
blue and royal purple, weaving them all into intricate twisted
leaf designs, or richly flower-bedecked cloths. Here was a little
stitched ship with embroidered sails poised for all time on the
crest of a scroll-like wave, and here a tree whose leaf would never
fall, and here a small bunched figure, like she or her Maries used
to be, who would stay for ever young.

There were elaborate anagrams woven round her name Marie
Stuarta. A crucifix with the word *undique* (on every side) symbolised that through the cross she was armed at all points. An
apple tree growing out of a thorn proclaimed through its motto
that her cause was increased by her captivity. The English diplomatist who saw an embroidered phoenix rising crowned from
flames with the legend 'En ma fin gêt mon commencement' tried
to puzzle out its political significance but gave up the riddle. It
was her mother's motto, 'In my End is my Beginning'.

This English diplomatist advised Cecil that 'few subjects
should be permitted to have access or conference with this lady;
for besides that she is a goodly personage (and yet in truth not

comparable to our Sovereign),' he is careful to add, 'she hath withal an alluring grace, a pretty Scotch accent, and a searching wit, clouded with mildness. Fame might move some to relieve her, and glory, joined to gain, might stir others to adventure much for her sake.'

She wrote to her ambassador in Paris, asking him to send her carnation satin as he would have a better choice in France than in London, with a pound of silver thread, the finest he could find. What he sent was too thick—'You are not a good chooser of silver thread', she playfully told him. She wanted the materials, and eight ells of carnation taffeta, to embroider an elaborate skirt for Elizabeth.

Her vain cousin was delighted with the gift and Mary, gratified by the warmth of her thanks, laid siege to the English Queen with a positive bombardment of presents, bracelets, headdresses, hoods from Paris, an elegant gold mirror to hang from her girdle, a complete set charmingly worked by herself including coif, collar and sleeves, network, even French sweetmeats. Elizabeth's thanks grew gradually more temperate until finally they chilled into the reminder of the difference in their ages— her cousin would have Mary remember that those who began to grow old were accustomed to take with two hands and give only with one finger.

Mary looked after her servants and attendants with her mother's loving care; her poor flock of wandering sheep she called them, humouring her dying secretary Roullet when, too ill to work, he became resentful and jealous of anyone who tried to fill his place. The affection between mistress and servant was reciprocal: the five thousand crowns she had given him for his services he left her when he died.

To her Cardinal uncle Mary wrote asking him to choose her another secretary. 'The qualifications of good temper are essential to my peace, and that of my household,' she wrote, 'where all are subjected to prison restraints, and confined within their own narrow little sphere, which render it expedient for them to be on friendly terms with each other; whereas, in consequence of poor Roullet's testiness and choleric disposition, there have been many affronts, jealousies and disputes for the last year, and nothing is so distressing to me as quarrels.'

She was in close correspondence with her uncle, the Cardinal of Lorraine. She might blame him for neglect in the administration of her dowry but the old relationship of revered uncle and submissive niece, preceptor and pupil, re-established itself as the years passed. It was a very necessary relationship for Mary. Carrying as she did a load of responsibility, she could look to him for support and guidance instead of having to provide them. There is a touching gratitude in her reply to a loving letter from him. 'To sum up, my kind uncle,' she was to write, 'I beg you to love me, and to command me as if I were your own daughter who loves you as herself.' She did not know as she penned those words in 1574 that death had already claimed the brilliant Prince of the Church, the uncle whose fertile brain had planned, designed and contrived for her in schemes both great and small. 'God bereaves me of one of the creatures I loved the best', she wrote, weeping, when she heard. 'What shall I say more? He has taken from me at one blow my father and my uncle. I shall follow, when it shall please Him, with the less regret.'

News penetrated, like the reverberation of distant thunder, into the fastness of the throneless Queen. Little Madame Ysabel died in far-away Spain in her twenty-third year. After weeping without knowing why, she lay still and remote in death as if in gentle slumber, and the prayers moving heavenwards from the earth for Mary Stewart thinned. Her middle-aged husband, Philip II, shut himself up in a monastery for a month to mourn the wife he loved so well.

Charles, her brother, the French King, died when he was

twenty-five, haunted by the memory of the St. Bartholomew's Day when the fate of thousands upon thousands of French Protestants was sealed—four thousand in Paris alone lost their lives in an orgy of slaughter.

Mary never freed herself from the illusion that some royal knight-errant would rise on her behalf in France or Spain. Hope rose as his brother Henri ascended the French throne—all her brothers-in-law had been fond of her but Henri used to be the one 'who loved me the best of all'.

Archbishop Hamilton was hanged by Lennox for being party to the King's murder. Lennox was murdered himself a few months later by vengeful Hamiltons to the cries of 'Remember the Archbishop!'

Master Knox, hollowed by words, declaimed his last sermon and, like an unlit lantern now life had deserted his shrunken soul-sheath, was laid to rest. He died at the eleventh hour one November night, his last words, 'Now it is come.'

She heard of Bothwell's reported death in Denmark three years before it actually took place, and made enquiries about a dying confession he was supposed to have made exonerating her of any part in Darnley's murder. But madness, which thirled his strong body, had already overtaken Bothwell, chained in his prison, and he died after ten years of captivity. Mary was to outlive him by nine years.

She must have wondered if she had ever ridden before the wind, if her heart had ever leapt at the sound of a footfall or thrilled at a touch, if there had ever been other days when she and her Maries looked for the love-glint in men's eyes. When she saw Mary Seton, she saw one who was old and grey and tired, with stiffening fingers that could no longer even guide a needle through her stitchery.

For seventeen years she shared her royal mistress's captivity until she was too ill to remain with her any longer. Her last days were spent in the convent at Rheims where Mary's Guise aunt was Abbess. Life must have seemed very long when Mary and her favourite Marie bade each other good-bye, as though they could never reach the end of it.

Her face was never still for she was ever biting at her lips and even in sleep it twitched. The damp and discomforts of her prisons had crippled her body, that wearied thwarted body which a lifetime ago Knollys and Scrope had warned Queen Elizabeth was so agile it might escape through her chamber window.

Religion alone coloured those outgoing years; from it Mary drew her only comfort and consolation to sustain her through the irking painfulness of her days. And now she no longer thought of herself as a woman undergoing personal privations and trials, but a woman called upon to suffer for her faith. It was not her own cross she carried, but the Cross of the Catholic Church. Her foes were its foes. For its sake she had to experience these inflictions; to serve it, strive so fiercely for deliverance from Protestant hands.

CHAPTER FOUR

Open the door and let me through.

FOR fifteen years the irascible Earl of Shrewsbury was Mary's reluctant gaoler, with eighty of his household servants and a band of forty men-at-arms to guard her. A certain respect outlasted the almost daily friction of such close and unnatural an association. Mary wrote to her Cardinal uncle that she did not believe her keeper would, for the honour of his house, allow any attempts on her life while she was in his charge; and when Queen Elizabeth asked Shrewsbury if any reliance could be placed on her cousin's word, he replied with vigour, 'I believe that if the Queen of Scotland promise anything, she will not break her word.'

Sir Ralph Sadler, who succeeded him, spoke of the Scots Queen's patience when they arrived at Tutbury in January to a dilapidated cold house with no comforts and few necessities, such as blankets or curtains and hangings to muffle the icy whistling draughts. 'Fair words and promises will not keep folk warm', he wrote to Cecil on their arrival. The mattress on the Queen's bed was found to be stained and smelling, and Mr. Somers, a co-guardian, gave her his, an ordinary featherbed. She was ill and lay on it so long the feathers came through the tick.

She was always in pain now with neuritis and rheumatism, her neck, arm and leg troubled her, and the old inflammation in her side. Her hair was cropped to make it easier for fomentations to be applied to relieve her severe headaches.

Elizabeth usually chose to have her moved to a still safer

prison in the depths of winter, probably because there was less danger of rescue during transit than in summer. Mary's guardians were not young men, and testy with gout, they found travelling under such severe conditions trying and arduous; but even these laboursome journeys had a beneficial effect on Mary's spirits after her pent up existence.

Accustomed all her life to exercise and the freedom of outdoor pursuits, the restraints of prison life exacted heavy toll. Sadler incurred his sovereign's bitter disapproval when he allowed the Scottish Queen, although she was strongly guarded, to accompany him to see his hawks fly. He vowed he would rather be shut up in the Tower all the days of his life than remain in his present charge.

Tutbury had always been an evil-omened place to Mary. In its rayless rooms, where mould furred the furniture and streaked the cracking walls, she had said good-bye to Mary Seton, her favourite Scots lady-in-waiting, and watched die her elderly favourite French attendant. Madame de Rallay had waited on the young Scots Queen in her laughing youth in France and sailed from her native country to share her captivity on foreign soil. At Tutbury the body of a priest, who had committed suicide to escape further persecution, was dangled outside Mary's windows, darkened by a high wall, for her to see.

Within the stillness of its damp confines she now learnt that her son had abandoned her. For an English pension, some dubious promises of the English succession and a gift of a dozen bloodhounds, he repudiated all his previous dealings with his mother and entered into a separate treaty with Queen Elizabeth.

It was so ominous that at first Mary could not believe it. She was his mother, an anointed Queen of Scotland, Dowager Queen of France—was she to be left by son and state, overlooked and forgotten as though she were some worthless thing, in ever-tightening durance? 'A mother's curse shall light upon him, I will deprive him of all the greatness to which through me he can pretend. He shall have nothing but what he inherits from his father.' 'Without him I am, and shall be of right, as long as I live, his Queen and sovereign, but he independently of me, can only be Lord Darnley or Earl of Lennox.' 'Without me, he is too insignificant to think of soaring.' But even as she penned the words that she alone could give him the legal right to bear the title of King, she must have known that nothing she could say, write or do could dislodge her son wedged on the throne of Scotland.

God and Queen Elizabeth at last answered Sir Ralph Sadler's prayer and he was relieved of his custodianship: his place was filled by the man who was to be Mary's last gaoler. Sir Amyas Poulet took over his new task at unhappy Tutbury. His puritanism was of that rigid stamp which, based on repression, finds outlet in harshness, cruelty and bigotry. He was as impervious to charm and graciousness as he himself was uncharming and ungracious. In his régime, captivity reached for Mary a galling intensity. Her instant antipathy to her new keeper can be understood when we read he informed her at their first interview that he would not be diverted from his duty for hope of gain, for fear of loss or any other respect whatsoever.

There is something curiously repellent about his reports of her health: 'The Scottish Queen is certainly in great pain, having defluxions (inflamed swellings) from rheumatic gout in her shoulder, her arm and her heel.' 'The Scottish Queen is getting a little strength, and is sometimes carried, in a chair, to one of the adjoining ponds to see the diversion of duck-hunting; but she is not able to walk without support on each side.' 'The lady is ill in one of her knees, but that is no new thing.'

Mary was next of kin to the English Queen—no one could deny her that, and the years that were passing over her in captivity were also shortening the Queen of England's span. If Elizabeth, the elder woman, died, a powerful party in England favourable to Mary would attempt to place her on the throne. But she was a Catholic, a menace to the established religion and the English nobility who did not favour her accession. Death alone could remove this danger, this Catholic heir-apparent with her potentialities, her unremitting claims and unceasing demands.

There were in England eager Catholic youths, and priests who would baulk at nothing, ready to deliver the Scots Queen. But no plots could form round her now for, through the vigilance of her puritan gaoler, she was cut off from all communication with the outside world. No letters or tidings could reach her, no whispers of promised relief penetrate to her in her new residence at Chartley, no pledges quicken her over-stored spirits.

When hopes were at their lowest, the unlooked-for happened and she found herself linked to her supporters. Through a man Gifford she received packets of letters hidden in the barrels of beer supplied to her household; through him she was able to pass out letters to be dispersed to her friends.

She accepted his credentials without hesitation and lavished rewards on him and the brewer for their services. She did not know, as she sat with her secretaries preparing missive after missive, inditing and directing, that each letter before it reached her from her ardent young confederates, each letter that left her hands, was read by unseen enemies who watched the gathering of the plot they themselves were fomenting, waiting until the evidence had accumulated and was complete.

All through spring her watchful guardian paid her his unsmiling visits, until one day in late summer he brought with him a welcome, unexpected invitation from a neighbouring nobleman who asked the Queen of Scots to grace his stag hunt with her presence. With blithe anticipation Mary and her confined household looked forward to the expedition. She thanked God He

had not yet set her so low, but that she was still able to handle
her cross-bow and gallop after the hounds on horseback.

The morning of the hunt dawned bright and fair. The air was
warm against their faces, but as yet the grass was grey with dew.
With her two secretaries, the master of her household, her physician, and two attendants carrying her cloak and bows and arrows, the Queen of Scots rode out, their voices calling to one
another, while her warder with his guard followed at some
distance.

So much happened within the next half hour, so great an up-
heaval of her unsuspecting thoughts took place, so many demands were made upon her, that it was as though in that short
space of time, every part of her being were summoned into play
to brace, shield and arm her.

She was cantering happily amongst her attendants when she
heard a voice accuse her of conspiring against Queen Elizabeth
and the state. For a moment her heart must have misgiven her,
but she denied the accusation roundly and promptly. She saw
her secretaries parted from her and her warder ride before her,
leading her to some unknown destination. With a horror unlike
anything else she had before experienced, she realised she was
not being taken back to Chartley, that the hunting expedition
had been a device to entice her, unthinking, from her quarters
that they might be searched in her absence. The thought of her
unburnt papers overwhelmed her. Springing from her horse, she
sat down on the ground and refused to go farther.

Words were not missiles—protests, prayers, threats, vanished
like vapour on the summer air as though they had never been.
Once more she was helped on to her mount and, appalled but
defiant, lead to Tixall.

For seventeen days she was kept, solitary, in her temporary
quarters, under Poulet's guard, during which time he refused to
speak a word to her, while at Chartley her papers, ciphers, seals

and jewels were seized. Elizabeth ordered that her caskets be sent to her, but any jewels that Mary had left were little more than trinkets, a few rings and chains. They found her books of household expenses—Sadler had spoken of her as a frugal good housewife, which she needed to be for she supported all her own servants on her dwindled dowry. They found also a sonnet written by her in French, whose translation reads:

> *Alas, what am I! What's my life become?*
> *A corse existing when the pulse hath fled;*
> *An empty shadow, mark for conflicts dread,*
> *Whose only hope of refuge is the tomb.*
>
> *Cease to pursue, O foes, with envious hate,*
> *My share of this world's glories hath been brief;*
> *Soon will your ire on me be satiate,*
> *For I consume and die of mortal grief.*
>
> *And ye, my faithful friends, who hold me dear,*
> *In dire adversity, and bonds, and woe,*
> *I lack the power to guerdon love sincere;*
> *Wish, then, the close of all my ills below,*
> *That purified on earth, with sins forgiven,*
> *My ransomed sould may share the joys of heaven.*

When she was taken from Tixall, the beggars, gathered at the gates, stretched out their craving hands for alms, but the woman on horseback, tears coursing down her cheeks, cried out as she passed them, 'I have nought for you, I am a beggar as well as you. All is taken from me.' A strong band of horsemen was waiting to guard her on her journey. 'Good gentlemen,' she said to them, entreaty in her voice, 'I am not witting or privy to anything against the Queen.' Unspeaking and unheeding, they fell in behind her, and the dolorous procession moved onwards, back to

her ransacked quarters at Chartley where her servants greeted
her with sobs and tears.

There was talk of removing her to the Tower in London but
that was too public a platform for Elizabeth and her ministers,
and she was conveyed to Fotheringay Castle, a strong fortress
with a double moat, in Northamptonshire. Mary had now
reached the final stage of the journey which began forty-four
years before in the palace of Linlithgow.

A trial was necessary to lend a legal aspect to the proceedings.
The French ambassador in the name of his King demanded that
the Queen of Scots be allowed counsel and all things necessary
for her defence. He received a verbal answer from Queen Elizabeth that the civil law considered persons in the situation of the
Scots Queen unworthy of counsel.

Mary's attitude was that she, an anointed Queen, was subject to no one but God, to Whom alone she was accountable for
her actions. She was willing to answer all things that might be
objected against her before a free and full Parliament (she knew
she had a following amongst the English nobility), but she refused to admit the authority of any lesser court. She agreed, however, to prove her goodwill, to answer the accusation that she
had plotted against her sister Queen's life, because she knew
the proceedings would be continued if she were absent. She
knew also she was already judged and condemned. 'I adjure you',
she warned Cecil and the Lord Chancellor, 'to look to your con-
sciences in this matter, for remember the theatre of the world is
wider than the realm of England.'

When she entered the great hall of Fotheringay that October
day, she was supported by her French physician on one side, and
her Scots master of the household on the other. She found,
awaiting her, their faces implacable as a wall, the great law officers of the crown, peers, privy counsellors and judges—English-

men all. 'Alas! how many counsellors are here,' she exclaimed, 'yet not one for me.'

For two days she fenced and held her own with the ablest brains in England. 'I came to England', was her unassailable beginning, 'to crave the aid that had been promised me, and it is well known that, contrary to all law and justice, I have been detained in prison ever since.' Her knowledge of English law was searching, and she had an answer for every question. When they produced copies of letters purporting to be written by her, she told them to bring her 'mine own hand-writ, anything to suit a purpose may be put in what are called copies.' 'My crimes', she stated, 'consist in my birth, the injuries that have been inflicted upon me, and my religion. Of the first, I am justly proud, the second I can forgive, and the third has been my sole consolation and hope under all my afflictions.' She spoke truly when she told them it was more in accordance with her nature to pray with Esther than to play the part of Judith. 'My lord,' she exclaimed to Cecil, 'you are my enemy.' 'Yes,' he replied, compact with antagonism, 'I am the enemy of all Queen Elizabeth's adversaries.'

She maintained throughout that she had longed for liberty and 'earnestly laboured to procure it. Nature impelled me to . . . I have written to my friends, and solicited them to assist me to escape from her (Elizabeth's) miserable prisons, in which she has kept me now nearly nineteen years, till my health and hopes have been cruelly destroyed.' But she called God to witness that she had never conspired the death of the Queen of England. She may have left the method of her deliverance to her Catholic advisers but she certainly knew that her deliverance was bound to include what the conspirators referred to amongst themselves as 'the principal execution'. It was Protestants versus Catholics, Catholics versus Protestants. The victory of one meant the extermination of the rival Queen, and Mary must have desired the death of the puissant Elizabeth even more heartily than Elizabeth desired that of her captive Mary.

She asked for an advocate to plead her cause, for one more day to be allowed for consideration and preparation of her defence. She was refused both. Then she rose from her seat to her full majestic height and demanded to be heard in Parliament in presence of the Queen of England and her Council. Abruptly the court broke up.

Sentence of death was passed on her four weeks later. She heard the intimation of it with composure; indeed the moment the bearers of it spoke of religion, she, and not they, was in command. They told her to confess and acknowledge her offences against their Queen; that the reason why her death was demanded by Elizabeth's subjects was because she was a competitor for her crown; that Elizabeth could have no security while she was alive for all the Catholics styled her their sovereign; and that, if she survived, Elizabeth's religion would not remain in security.

'I thank God and you for the honour you do me', she was swift to answer, 'in regarding me as an instrument for the reestablishment of my religion in this isle, of which, however unworthy, I will undertake to be a zealous defender, and will cheerfully shed my blood in that cause.'

'It is a fine thing', they said, taken aback, 'for you to make yourself out a saint and a martyr; but you shall be neither, as you are to die for plotting the murder and deposition of our Queen.'

'I am not so presumptuous as to pretend to honours of saint and martyr,' she returned; 'but although you have power over my body, by the Divine permission, you have none over my soul, nor can you prevent me from hoping that, by the mercy of God Who died for me, my blood and life will be accepted as offerings freely made by me for the maintenance of His Church.'

No indignity was spared her. She heard them working in the

hall, erecting the scaffold. Her room and even her bed were hung with mourning, to signify that already she was a dead woman. On the orders of Elizabeth, her canopy (the mark of royalty) was knocked down, that she be deprived of the honours and dignity of a Queen. Poulet covered his head in her presence and, refusing to address her with her royal title, referred to her as 'this lady'.

She wrote to her faithful Archbishop Beaton in Paris, recommending her poor servants to him, in the name of God. 'Console them of your charity, for in losing me they lose everything . . . Adieu! for the last time. Be mindful of the soul and honour of her who has been your Queen, mistress and good friend.'

In her last letter to Elizabeth she denied having borne her malice or cherished murderous intentions against her. She entreated her to prevent her from being poisoned or secretly assassinated, 'not from fear of the pain, which I am ready to suffer, but on account of the reports they would circulate of my death.' Mary's dread was that her enemies would impute to her the crime of suicide, or pretend she had confessed guilt or been unfaithful to her religion. That was why she desired her servants to be present at her death, 'to remain the witnesses and attestators of my end, my faith in my Saviour, and obedience to His Church . . . From Fotheringay this 19th of December, 1586. Your sister and cousin wrongfully a prisoner, Marie Royne.'

The English Queen shed tears when she read this letter, but she wrote bitterly through her secretaries to Mary's guardians, complaining that they had not rid the world of their charge by having her secretly murdered. The puritan Poulet refused to make so foul a shipwreck of his conscience by doing any such thing. It was more than three months before Queen Elizabeth could bring herself to sign the warrant for the execution, and she only did so when she realised that her statesmen had no intention of saving her the inculpation of her signature. There is a theory that she never signed the warrant, that her ministers, alarmed at her procrastination, caused her signature to be forged. For weeks after the execution, Cecil did not dare come near Queen Elizabeth.

The Earl Marshal, who was the Earl of Shrewsbury, and the Earl of Kent broke the communication to the Scots Queen that on the morrow she was to die. She remarked that she had not thought the Queen her sister would ever have consented to her death, but God's will be done. It was reported to Cecil how she heard the news: 'She seemed not to be in any terror, for anything that appeared by her outward gesture or behaviour, but rather, with smiling cheer and pleasing countenance, digested and accepted the admonition of preparation to her unexpected execution, saying "that her death should be welcome unto her".'

When she, the smile still faint upon her face, was left alone with her attendants and servants, they came round her, weeping and kissing her hands. 'Now, then, take it patiently', she told them. She busied herself making provision for them to return to France and Scotland, arranging the little money she had in her possession into different bundles for them. She asked them to pray for her and climbed on to her bed.

They knelt on the floor, their beads heavy in their hands, praying until the agitated air in the shrouded room hung with words and the sobbing intake of their breath. Two or three times an unquiet silence passed over the mourning figures as they listened for some movement to come from the woman on the bed. She lay so still they thought she too must be praying and once more their fingers felt for their beads.

At six in the morning she told her attendants she had but two hours to live, and bade them dress her as for a festival. She had long been denied her almoner, and entered her oratory alone, kneeling at the miniature altar where he had been accustomed to celebrate mass.

The Sheriff with his white wand entered her bedchamber where she and her attendants knelt in prayer. 'Madam,' he said, and his voice wavered, 'the Lords have sent me for you.' Mary turned her face towards him. 'Yes,' she replied, 'let us go.'

She could not walk alone, but her servants said there was one thing they could not and would not do—lead her to the scaffold, although they would wait upon her to her last sigh and were prepared to die with her. Two of Poulet's servants were appointed to assist her.

She passed from her chamber through the entry into the great hall up to the scaffold. She answered steadfastly the Protestant Dean of Peterborough, who called on her to change her opinion and repent, 'Mr. Dean, I am settled in the ancient Catholic Roman religion, and mind to spend my blood in defence of it.' When he would have pressed her further, she replied, 'Mr. Dean, trouble not yourself any more, for I am settled and resolved in this my religion, and am prepared therein to die.' He began to pray, but she resolutely and with vehemence prayed through him in Latin.

The executioners knelt before her and asked her to forgive them her death. 'I forgive you with all my heart,' she answered readily, 'for now, I hope, you shall make an end of all my troubles.'

She started to disrobe hurriedly as though anxious to be gone. An executioner grasped from her neck the Agnus Dei as his perquisite but she took it out of his hands and gave it to one of her women, telling him he would be given money for it. He with his fellow and her two women took off her chain of pomander beads and some of her apparel. 'I never had such grooms to make me unready,' she told them, smiling, 'and never did I put off my clothes before such a company.'

Still smiling, she suffered her eyes to be bound and with no token of hesitancy knelt on the cushion. Uttering the words, 'In manus tuas Domine me commendo', her hands thrummling for the block, she bent down that pilgrim head which had lain on so many pillows.

MARY
Queen of Scots

✳

Index

INDEX

HENRY VII.

ELIZAB

TUDOR

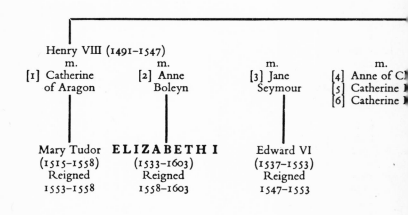

Henry VIII (1491–1547)
m.   m.   m.   m.
[1] Catherine   [2] Anne   [3] Jane   [4] Anne of Cl
of Aragon   Boleyn   Seymour   [5] Catherine
                                           [6] Catherine

Mary Tudor   **ELIZABETH I**   Edward VI
(1515–1558)   (1533–1603)   (1537–1553)
Reigned   Reigned   Reigned
1553–1558   1558–1603   1547–1553

m.
[1] Francis [II of
(1544–15

Simplified Tree showing
relationship between
Mary of Scotland and
Elizabeth of England

Jame